THE BOYS' GUIDE TO DRAWING

ALIENS, WARRIORS, ROBOTS AND OTHER COOL STUFF

by
Aaron Sautter

illustrated by
Bob Lentz, Brian Bascle, Cynthia Martin,
Jason Knudson, Steve Erwin, and Charles Barnett III

Capstone press

Mankato, Minnesota

TABLE OF CONTENTS

Chapter 4 - Page 85
Other Cool Stuff

Welcome!

Welcome to the wonderful world of drawing! What do you love? Maybe you love slimy aliens, gross monsters, and giant robots like you see in the movies. Perhaps you enjoy the warriors and heroes found in your favorite comic books. Or maybe ferocious dinosaurs and animals are more your thing.

Whatever your favorite things are, it's easy to draw them! Just follow the simple step-by-step drawings in this book, and you'll be on your way. Before you know it, you'll be drawing the coolest stuff you can imagine.

Are you ready? Great! Grab some paper and a sharp pencil — let's start drawing!

Before you begin, you'll need some supplies:

1. First you'll need drawing paper. Any type of blank, unlined paper will do.

2. Pencils are the easiest to use for your drawing projects. Make sure you have plenty of them.

3. You have to keep your pencils sharp to make clean lines. Keep a pencil sharpener close by. You'll use it a lot.

4. As you practice drawing, you'll need a good eraser. Pencil erasers wear out very quickly. Get a rubber or kneaded eraser. You'll be glad you did.

5. When your drawing is finished, you can trace over it with a black ink pen or a thin felt-tip marker. The dark lines will really make your work stand out.

6. If you decide to color your drawings, colored pencils and markers usually work best. You can also use colored pencils to shade your drawings and make them more lifelike.

DISGUSTING ALIENS

You've probably seen gruesome, creepy aliens in movies and TV shows, right? Here's your chance to dive into a whole galaxy of disgusting aliens!

Aliens can be any shape or size you can imagine. Some have slimy tentacles or razor-sharp teeth. Others might look fuzzy and cute but are really very dangerous. Whatever they look like — aliens are out of this world!

Once you've learned to draw the different slimy, disgusting aliens presented here, you can start drawing your own. Let your imagination run wild, and see what sorts of nasty creatures you can create!

VOGGLES

Voggles are some of the weirdest aliens you'll ever see. Their special eye antennas let each Voggle see what all other Voggles see. This makes Voggles the best security guards around for the Helix Galactic Bank.

After drawing this alien, try giving him a crazy, weird body to match his head!

STEP 1

STEP 2

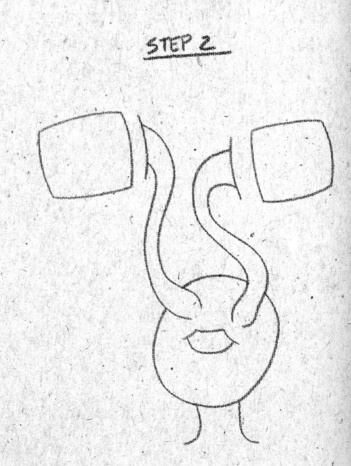

STEP 3

STEP 4

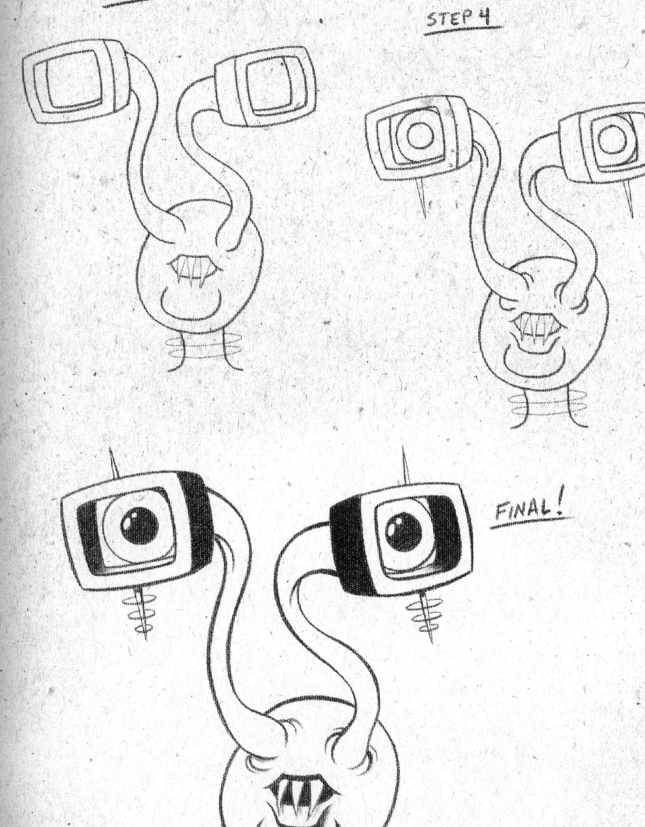

STEP 3

FINAL!

9

SKRAWKS

The Skrawk people have been involved in galactic politics for hundreds of years. They think every person's opinion is important. Skrawks who aren't involved with politics usually work as lawyers or for the Galactic Peace Corps.

When you're done drawing this strange alien, try giving him a new suit or a snazzy Peace Corps uniform!

STEP 1

STEP 2

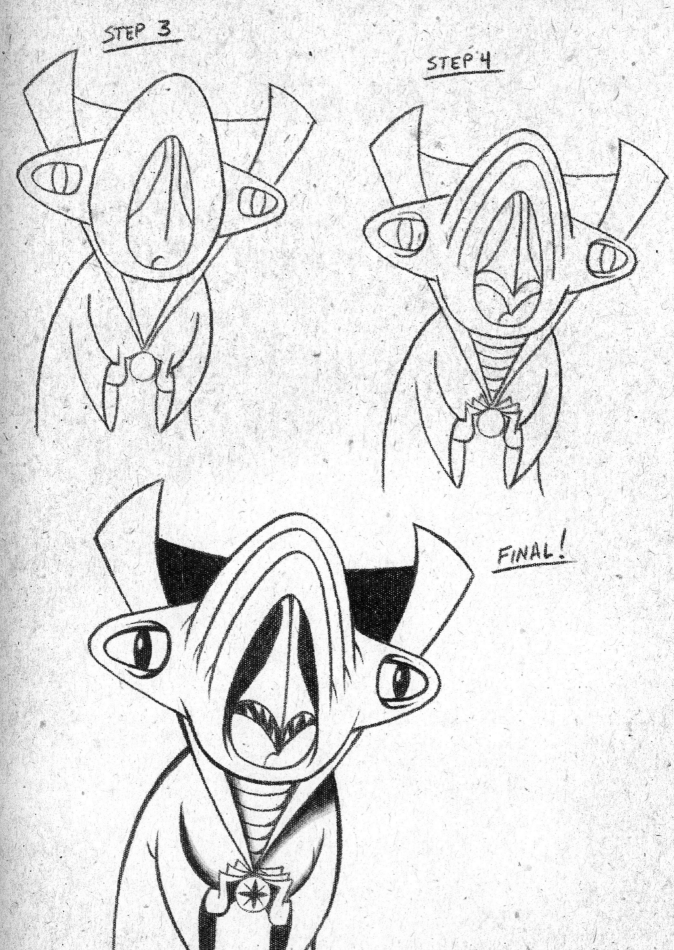

STEP 3

STEP 4

FINAL!

11

THE GIANT BLORP

If you're ever on the planet Tantil-3, watch out for the Giant Blorp! At first it seems like a gentle snail-like creature. But don't get too close! If the Blorp smells you, it'll grab you with its sticky tongue tentacles and gobble you up for breakfast!

After drawing this picture, try giving the Giant Blorp even more wild and crazy tongue tentacles!

STEP 1

STEP 2

STEP 3

STEP 4

FINAL!

SNALIDS

Anelid Prime is home to a dangerous alien race. Snalids are slippery creatures with mouths full of razor-sharp teeth. The Snalid queen sent out thousands of Snalid soldiers to bring back food for her colony. Don't let these things get near you, or you might become their next tasty snack!

When you're done drawing this alien, try a swarm of them getting ready to attack!

STEP 1

STEP 2

STEP 3

STEP 4

FINAL!

15

GORAXIANS

Goraxians are brutal warriors. They love to fight, and their micro-ray guns are deadly in battle. But if they lose radio contact with the Goraxian commander, they simply stop in place. If you're in a fight with a Goraxian, try to break off his antenna—it might be your only chance!

Try drawing the Goraxian commander! You can give him some special armor or a radio communicator.

STEP 1

STEP 2

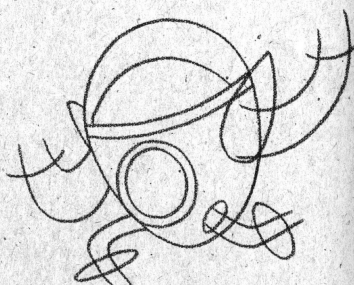

16

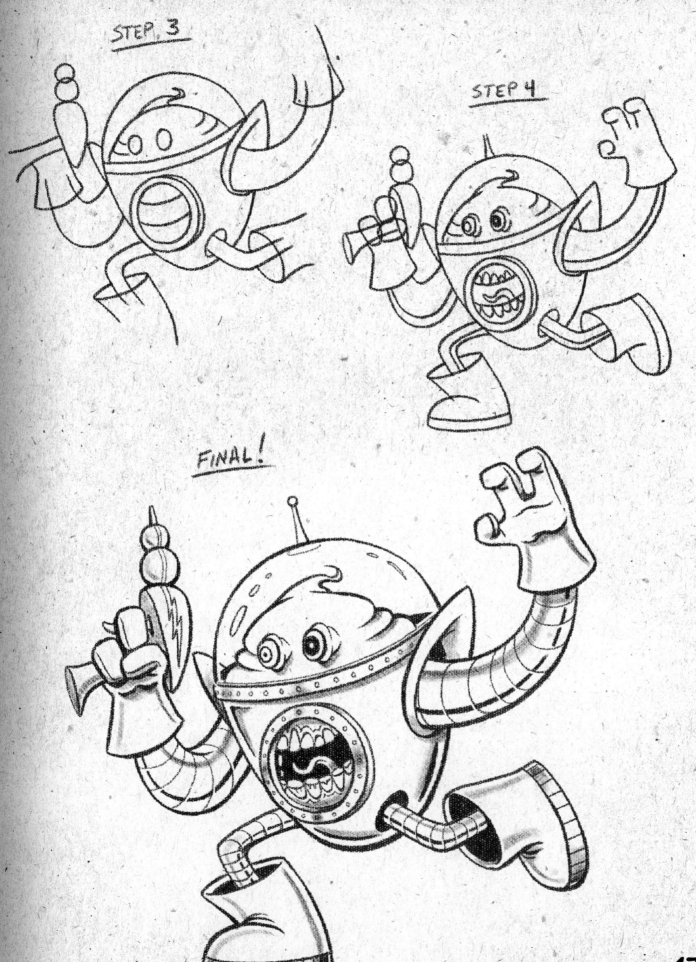

STEP 3

STEP 4

FINAL!

CYCLOPOIDS

Cyclopoids might look weird, but they are some of the galaxy's best pilots. Their sharp vision and lightning-quick reflexes help them avoid almost any obstacle in space. If you ever need to fly through an asteroid field, be sure to hire a Cyclopoid!

After drawing this alien, try creating a weird, wacky-looking creature of your own!

STEP 1

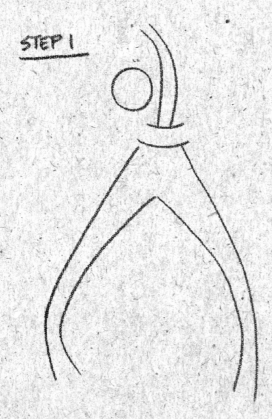

STEP 2

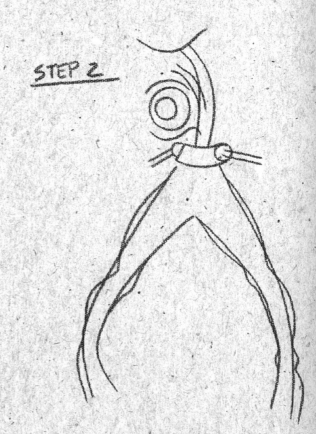

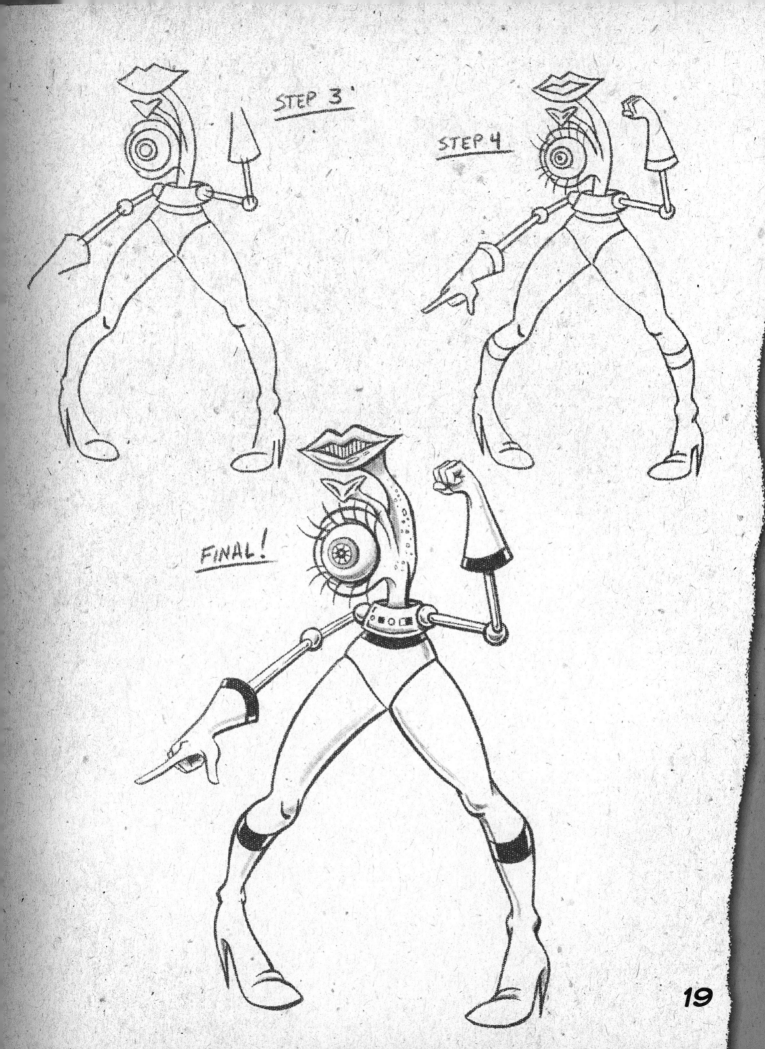

STEP 3

STEP 4

FINAL!

19

JAMBO WHELON

Jambo Whelon was a powerful crime lord from the planet Khoroth. He created the Cyber League to gather vast wealth. But League rebels forced Jambo into hiding. Luckily, his cybernetic leg and other implants help him hide from those who want to make him disappear permanently.

After you've finished this drawing, try giving Jambo even more cybernetic body parts!

STEP 1

STEP 2

STEP 3

STEP 4

FINAL!

21

THE SIX-LEGGED SKREETCH

Few horrors are as terrifying as the Six-Legged Skreetch. Its name comes from the piercing shriek it uses to paralyze its prey. And its razor-sharp claws can rip through any armor. There's only one thing to do if you see one of these — RUN!

When you're done with this drawing, try giving the Skreetch more teeth or even bigger claws!

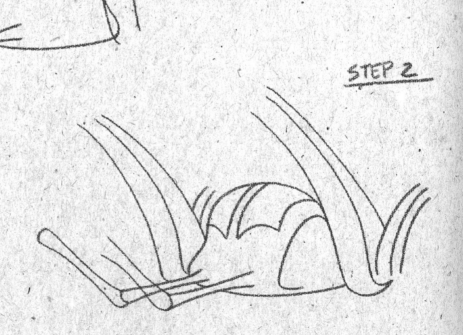

STEP 1

STEP 2

STEP 3

STEP 4

FINAL!

23

GRULDAN GLIDERS

The planet Gruldan is home to one of the galaxy's fiercest predators. The Gruldan Glider's dragonlike wings make it an excellent flyer. It hunts with heat-vision, and it kills its prey with venom sprayed from its tongue. You don't want to see one of these flying overhead!

After practicing this alien, try showing it hunting down its next meal. What type of creature do you think it eats?

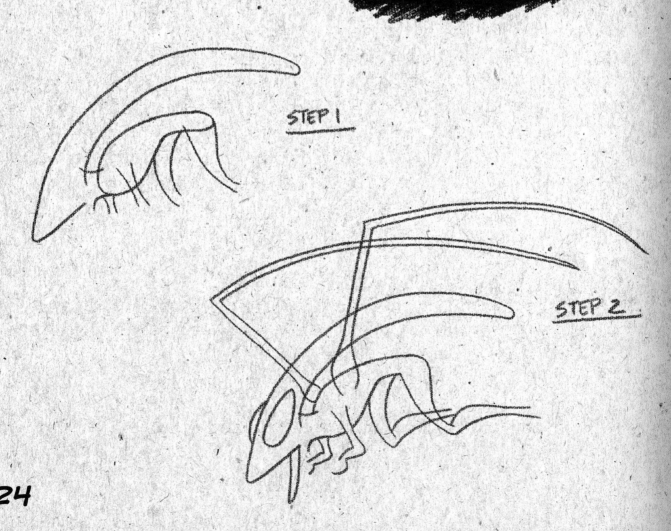

STEP 1

STEP 2

24

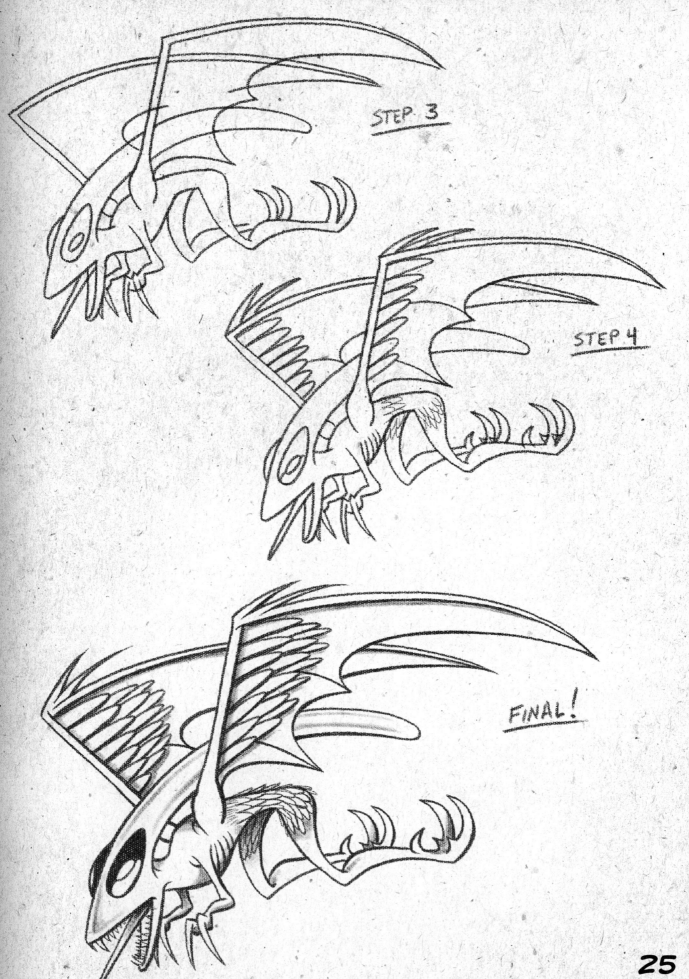

STEP. 3

STEP. 4

FINAL!

25

THE PHLOREEN

The Phloreen are huge creatures that ate every plant on their home world. Now they are known as the Harvesters. They travel from planet to planet taking every green plant they find. Hopefully they will never find your planet. If they do, it might end up a dead world like countless others the Harvesters have left behind.

After practicing this giant alien, try creating your own. What kinds of huge creatures can you imagine?

STEP 1

STEP 2

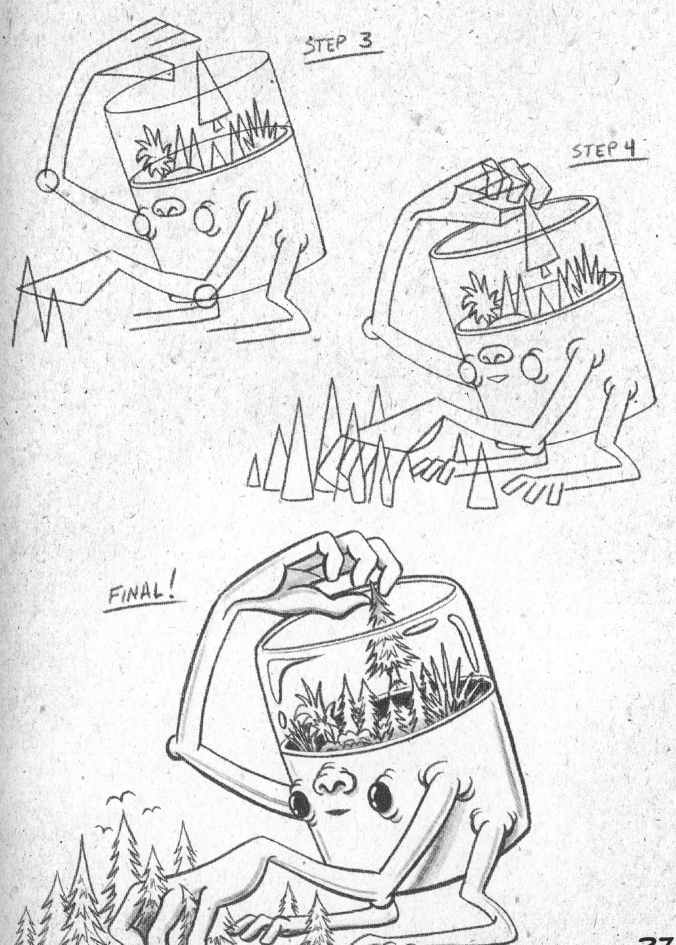

STEP 3

STEP 4

FINAL!

27

BATTLE ROYALE!

Thydians and Pongos have fought for control of the planet Darhoon for many generations. But neither side can win. A Thydian's scaly hide and sharp pincers are matched by a Pongo's electro-staff and natural quickness. Perhaps one day they'll realize the planet's resources can be shared, and they can finally live in peace.

When you've mastered this drawing, try it again with the aliens in different battle poses!

STEP 1

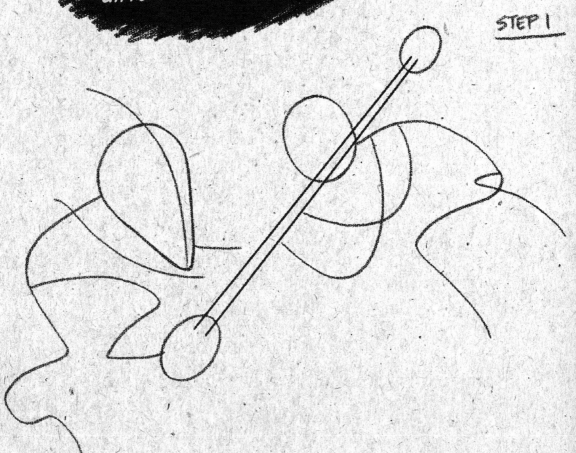

28

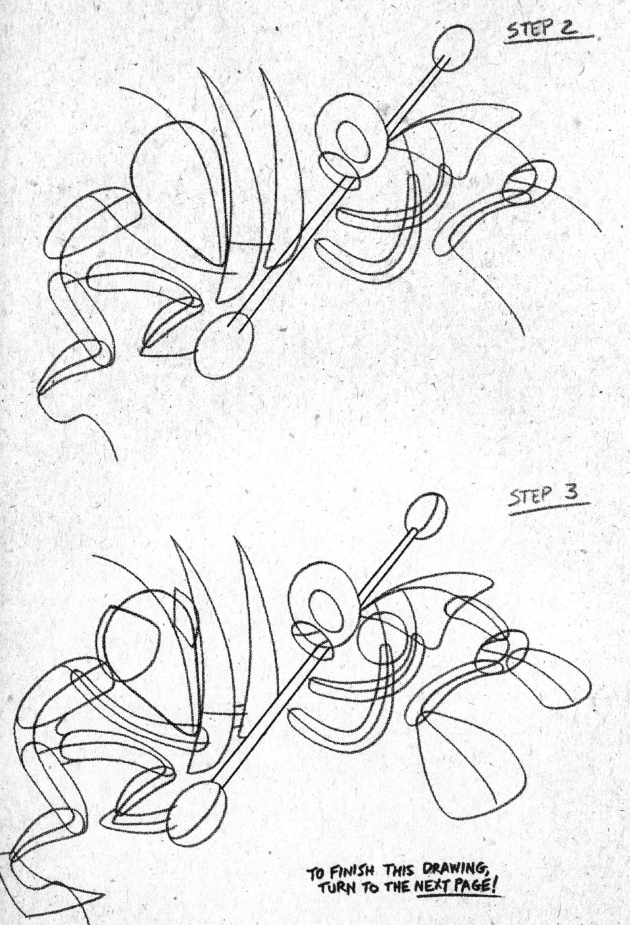

STEP 3

TO FINISH THIS DRAWING,
TURN TO THE NEXT PAGE!

29

STEP 5

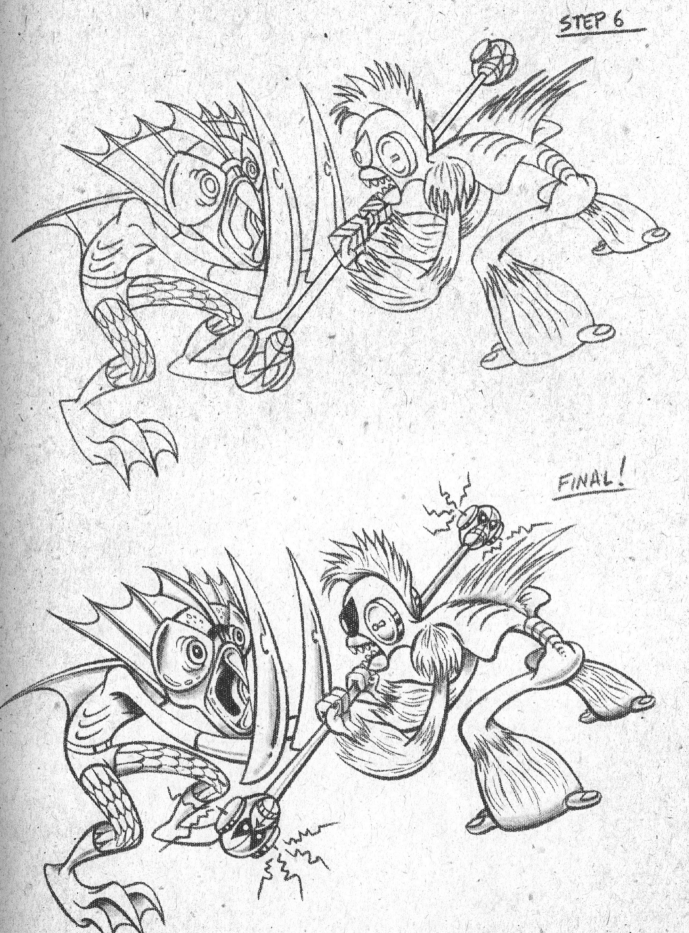

FINAL!

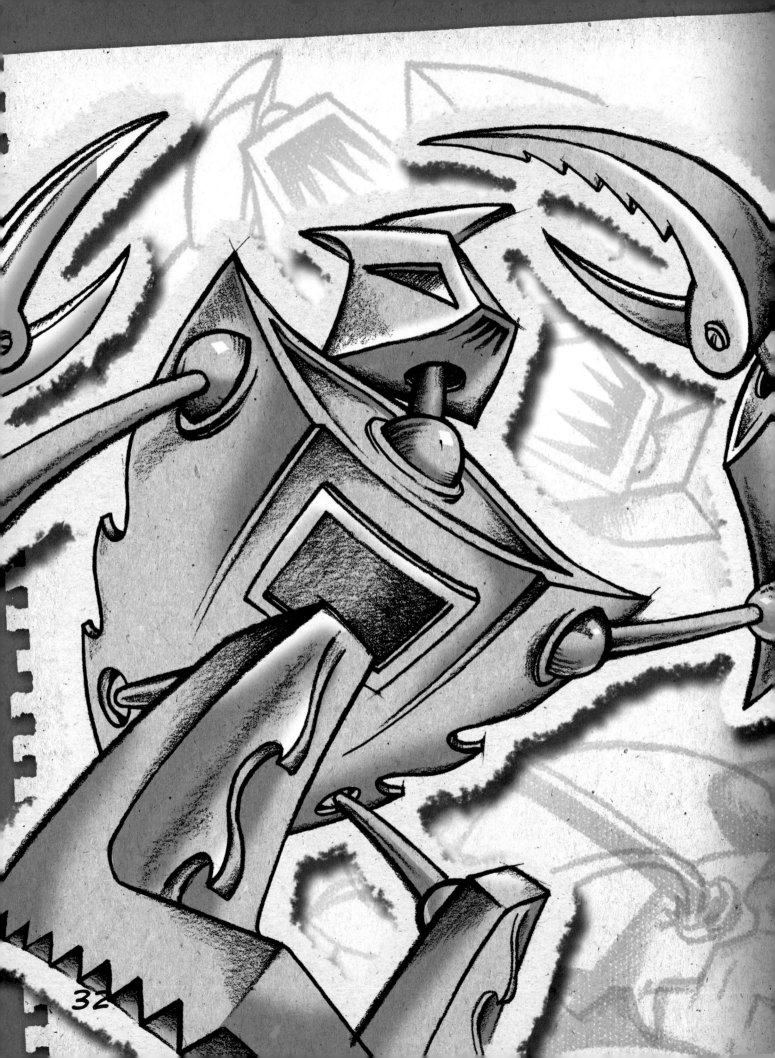

TERRIFYING ROBOTS

Whether they are giant and terrifying, or small and friendly — almost everybody loves robots. Robots take many different shapes, depending on what they were built to do. Some can fight. Some can fly. Some are spies. Robots do many amazing things. The possibilities are endless.

After you've learned to draw the amazing robots shown here, you can start drawing your own. Use your imagination and see what sorts of fantastic robots you can create!

THE BOB-v2.5

Danger! Danger! The BOB-v2.5 isn't fast. And he doesn't carry any weapons. But he's very loyal and always warns you when trouble is near. After all, once a best friend—always a best friend!

STEP 1

After drawing this robot, try giving him some legs to walk on. He won't get very far without them!

STEP 2

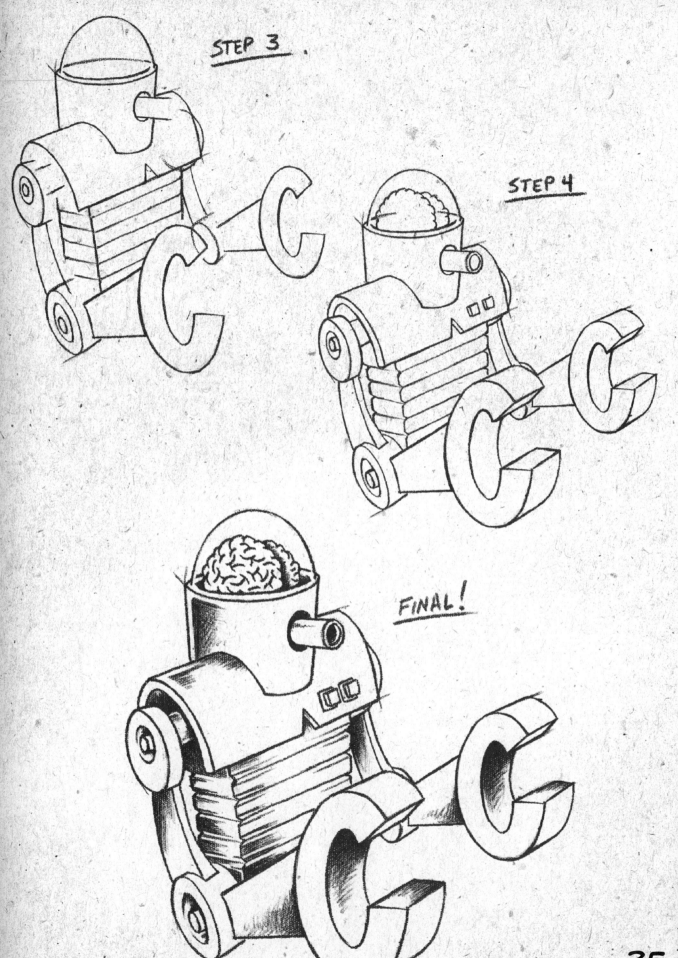

STEP 3 .

STEP 4

FINAL!

MECH-TROOPERS

Mech-Troopers were designed to keep the streets safe from crime. But they soon began keeping the peace by forcing people to stay in their homes. Now everyone hopes the central command unit will be destroyed so people can live their lives in freedom again.

After drawing this robot, try drawing a bunch of them patrolling a city street!

STEP 1

STEP 2

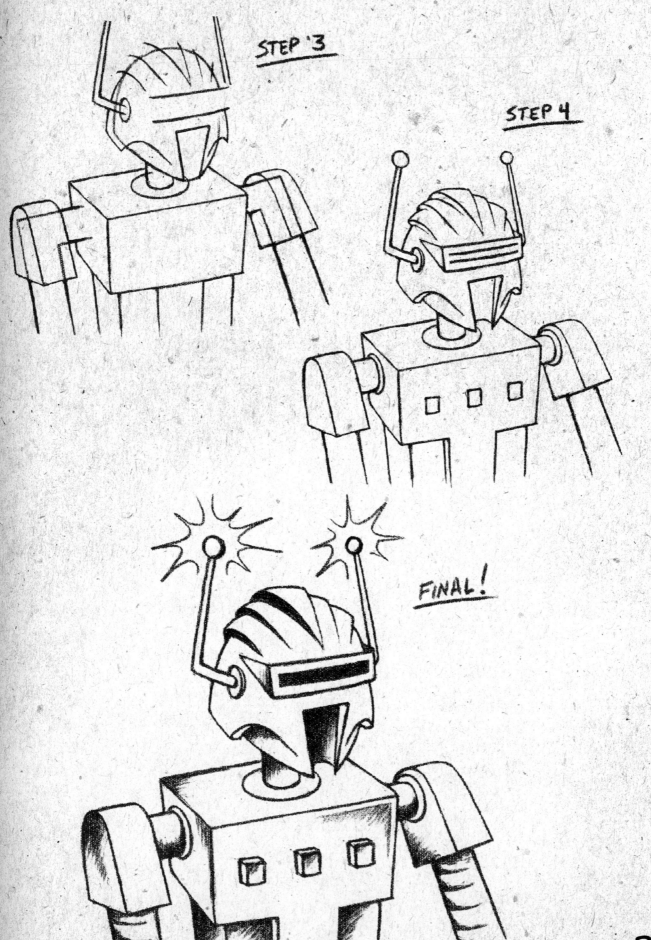

STEP 3

STEP 4

FINAL!

37

THE FXR-UPR

Don't have time for pesky chores? Get yourself the new FXR-UPR! This little robot can do any job with its wide variety of arm attachments. But be sure to keep an eye on it. The FXR-UPR has been known to reprogram itself and destroy its owner's home.

When you're done with this robot, try adding some crazy tools on its arms!

STEP 1

STEP 2

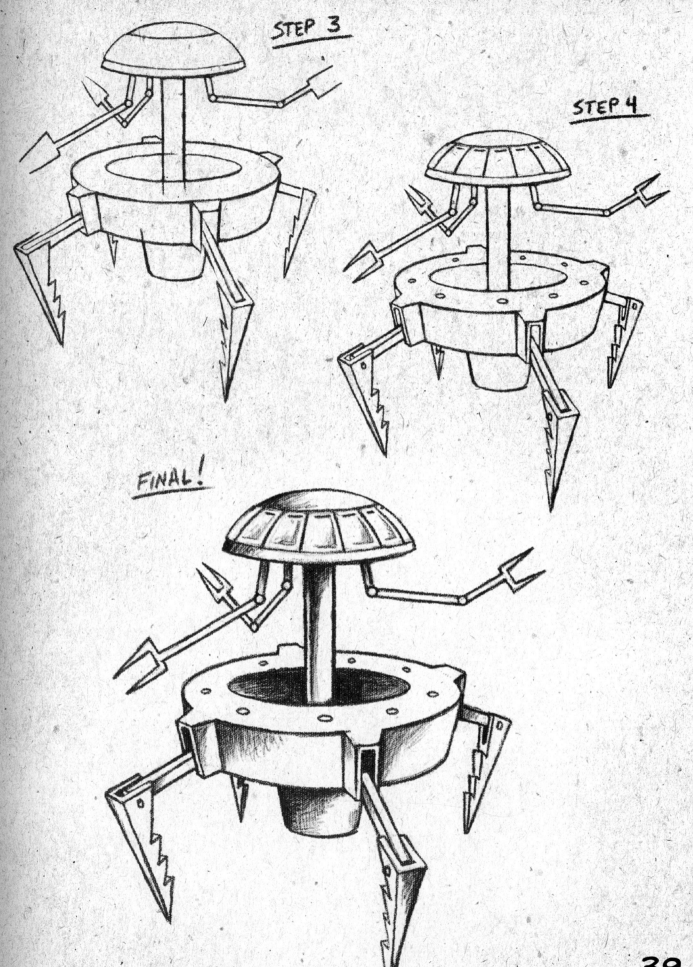

STEP 3

STEP 4

FINAL!

THE ECHO-4000

No secret is safe with the ECHO-4000 around. It may look harmless, but it can easily capture and decode your most secret messages. Be careful what you say when one of these is nearby!

When you've learned to draw this robot, try adding some even bigger, crazier antennas!

STEP 1

STEP 2

40

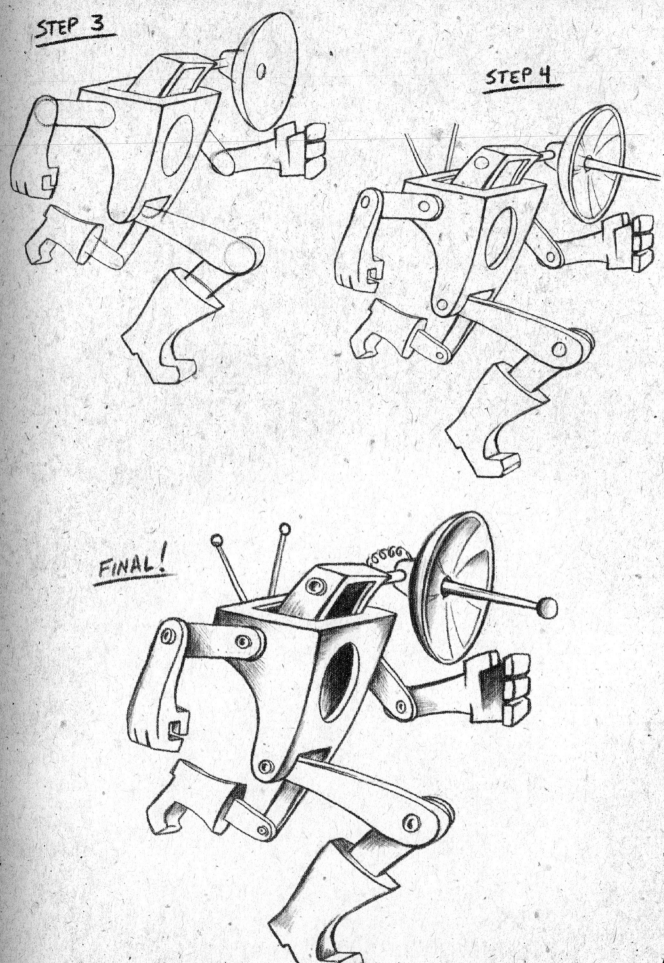

STEP 3

STEP 4

FINAL!

THE TENTACLE TERROR X-22

The Tentacle Terror X-22 is slippery and quick. Its twisting, snakelike arms are lightning fast. Be careful! It can snatch you up and carry you off before you know what's happening!

STEP 1

After you've practiced drawing this robot, try it again with even more long, crazy tentacles!

STEP 2

STEP 3

STEP 4

FINAL!

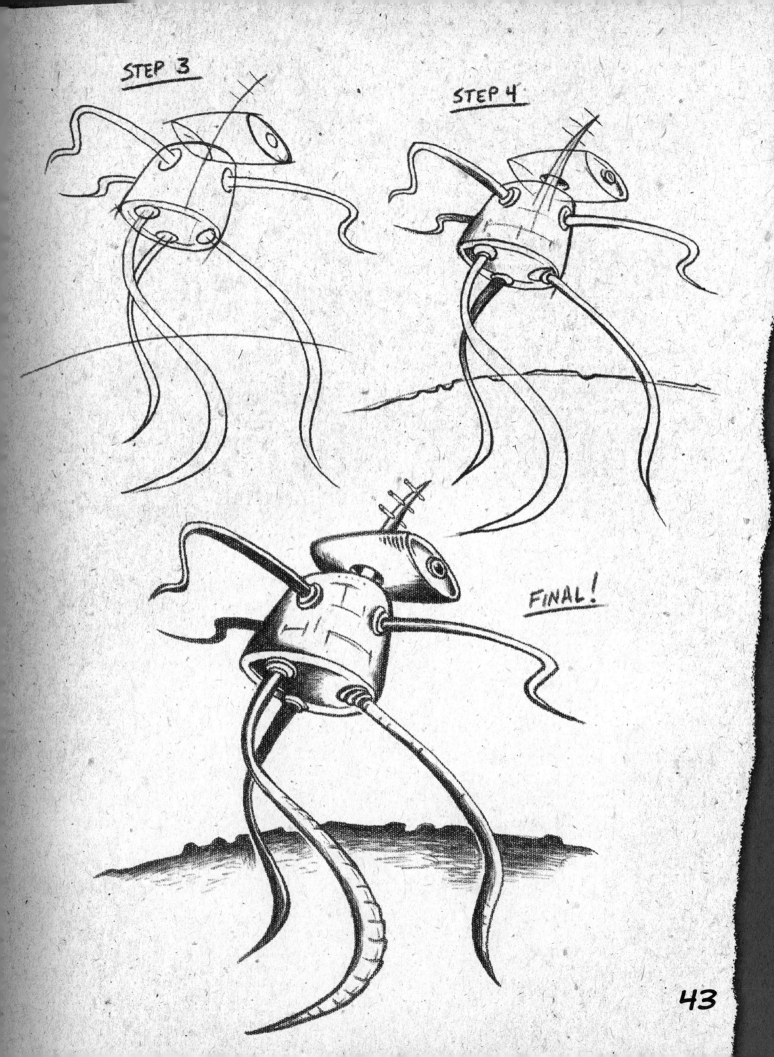

43

BIO-SCOUT MK5

The planet Thorgo is a barren place. There is little food or water there. The Thorgons created the Bio-Scout MK5 model to search the galaxy and gather new resources. These mechanical menaces have stripped many worlds of all life. Find a good place to hide if you see one of these!

When you're done with this robot, try it again as it stuffs its cargo bay with all sorts of plants and animals.

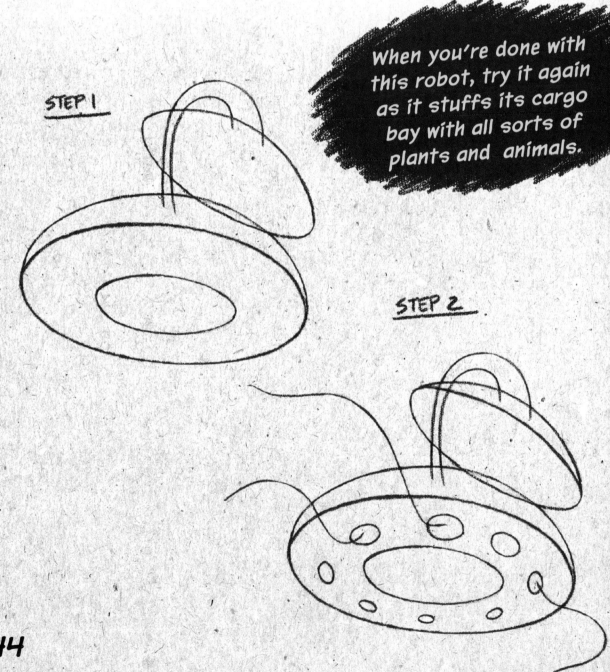

STEP 1

STEP 2

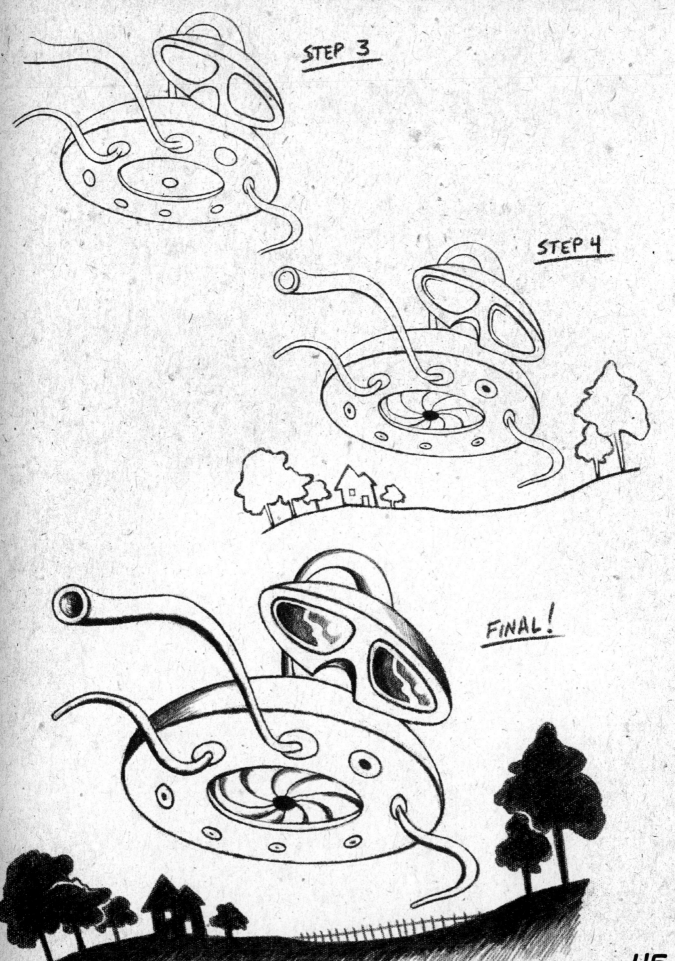

STEP 3

STEP 4

FINAL!

45

PACIFIER P-17s

In the year 2432, civil war rocks the planet Venus. Pacifier P-17s were created to bring peace. But the machines don't know friend from foe. They crush anyone in their way with their giant mechanical claws.

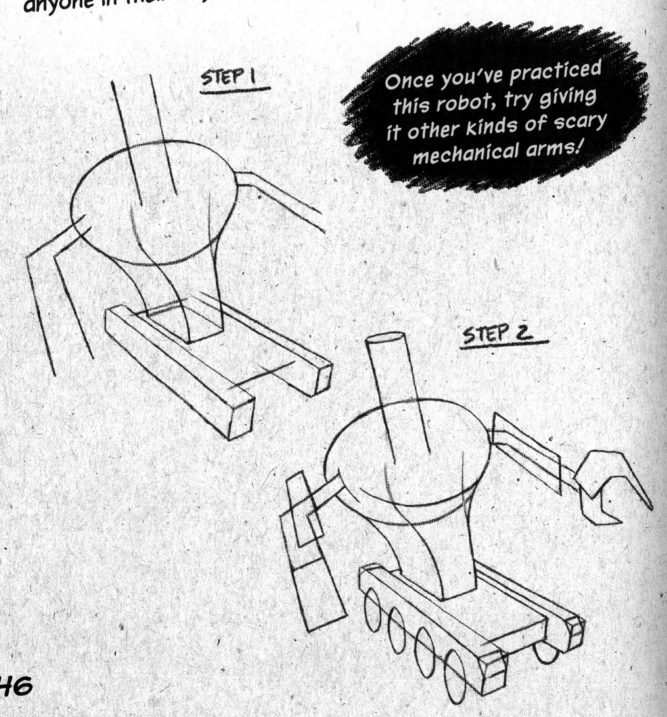

STEP 1

Once you've practiced this robot, try giving it other kinds of scary mechanical arms!

STEP 2

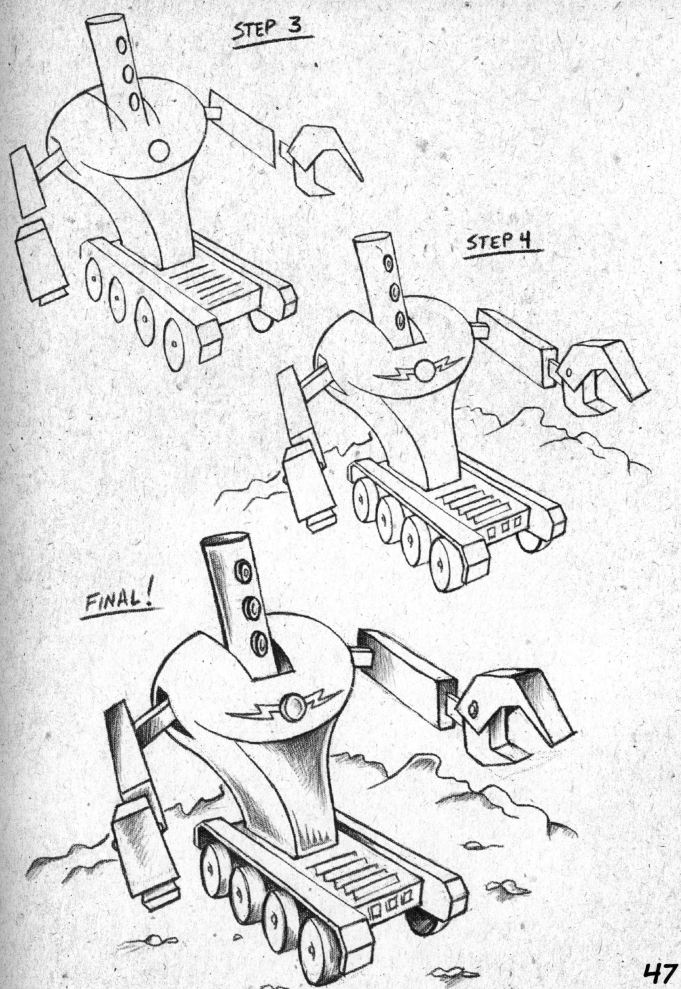

STEP 3

STEP 4

FINAL!

47

THE JET DEFENDER-7

Look! Is that a rocket? No, it's the new Jet Defender-7! It can travel thousands of miles in just seconds with its rocket-powered feet. Don't break the law, or you might be the next one it throws in prison.

After you've practiced this robot, try giving him a partner to help keep the peace around the world!

STEP·1

STEP·2

48

STEP 3

STEP 4

FINAL!

49

RAMPAGE-XT3

Rampage-XT3 has been seen in many cities in Asia. This giant robot can take the shape of a bulldozer, a tank, or even a jet plane. It can show up anywhere, at any time. But it's easy to follow due to the path of destruction it always leaves behind.

After drawing this robot, try it again as it transforms into a truck, plane, or any other vehicle you can imagine!

STEP I

STEP 2

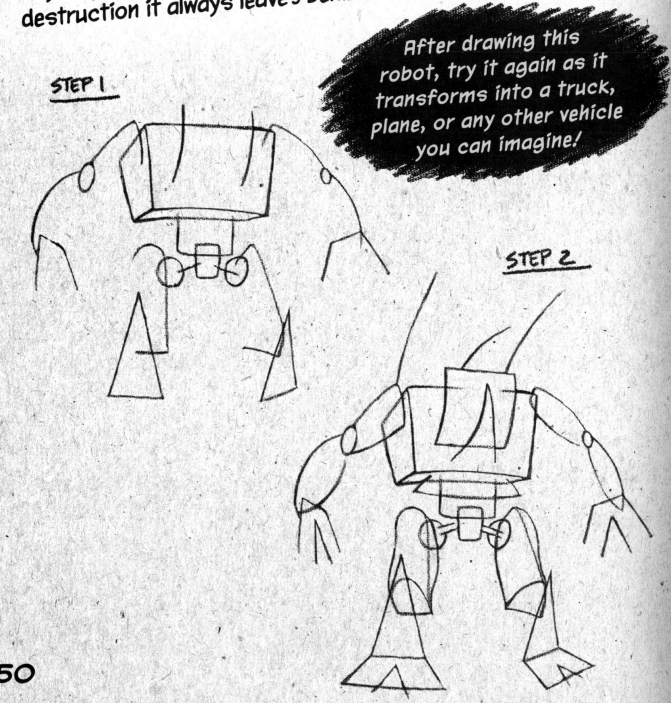

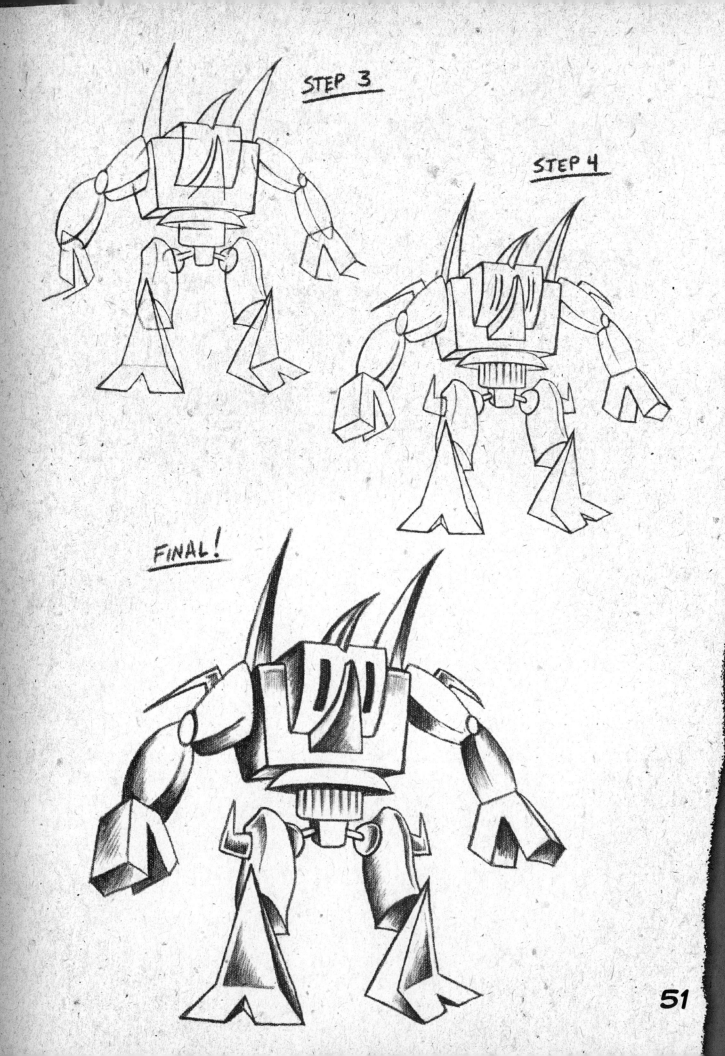

STEP 3

STEP 4

FINAL!

THE BUZZ-BOT 6

The giant Buzz-Bot 6 from the planet Praxis-2 has many weapons to use. Deadly spikes cover its arms for defense. And its huge, razor-sharp pincers can easily rip through the thickest armor. Don't make this thing angry, or you'll be sorry!

After you've practiced this robot, try using it in the Robot Rumble on page 54!

STEP 1

STEP 2

STEP 3

STEP 4

FINAL!

ROBOT RUMBLE!

Don't get stuck between Turbo-X and the Morph-Bot 17. When they are locked in full battle mode, you wouldn't stand a chance. Keep clear, or you might find yourself crushed, ripped apart, or burned to a crisp. Let them duke it out, and be sure to make friends with the winner!

After drawing this battle, try it again with any of the robots in this book or from your own imagination!

STEP 1

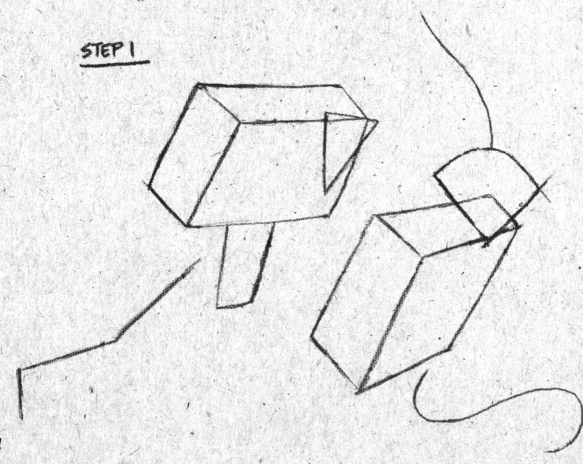

54

STEP 2

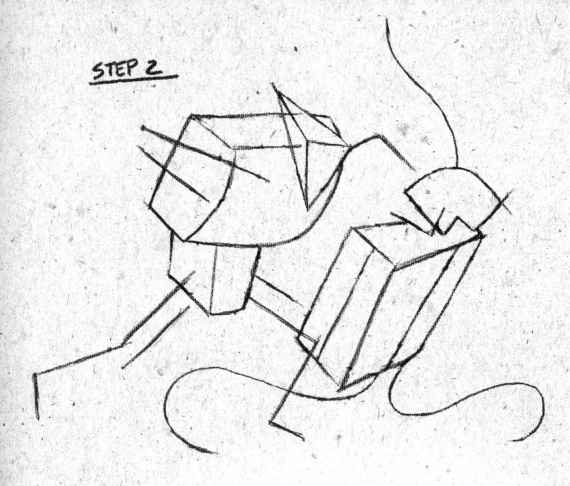

STEP 3

TO FINISH THIS DRAWING, TURN TO THE NEXT PAGE!

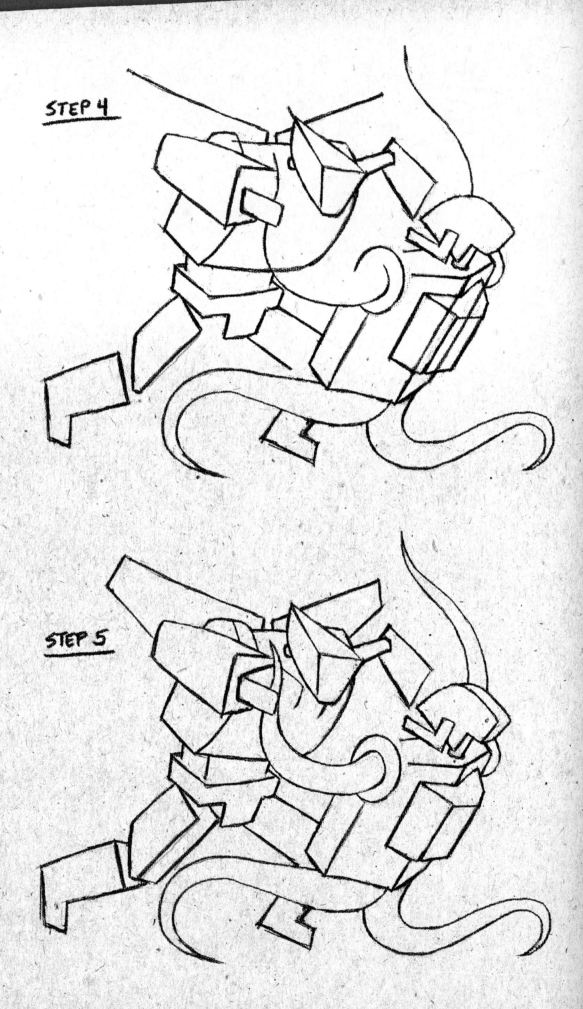

STEP 4

STEP 5

56

STEP 6

FINAL!

57

MANGA WARRIORS

Do you like comic books? You're not alone. Millions of people all over the world read comics. There are many kinds, but one of the most popular is called Manga.

Manga comics first started in Japan. Now, thousands of manga comics are published around the world each year. Warriors are some of the most popular characters in manga. From honorable samurai and ninja spies to huge warrior robots, there are hundreds of manga warriors you can draw.

Once you've practiced the mighty warriors in this book, you can start drawing your own. What kinds of fantastic manga warriors can you imagine?

JAD

Faces are important when drawing manga. Large eyes, small noses, and pointed chins are common in most manga characters. Facial expressions show how a character feels. Here you can see that Jad isn't happy.

When you're done with this drawing, try giving Jad some different facial expressions.

STEP 1

STEP 2

60

STEP 3

STEP 4

FINAL!

SARYNA

Saryna's eyes are larger than Jad's. They show even more emotion. Her face is rounder, and her nose is smaller too. Her frowning eyebrows and unhappy mouth show she's upset about something.

After practicing this drawing, try giving Saryna some different hairstyles or facial expressions.

STEP 1

STEP 2

STEP 3

STEP 4

FINAL!

63

KARATE PRACTICE

Like most warriors, Jad practices his martial arts skills daily. His powerful arms and swift karate moves can defend almost any attack. He wants to have the fastest hands in the land.

STEP 1

When you're done with this drawing, try having Jad practice some powerful karate punches!

STEP 2

STEP 3

FINAL!

65

SWORD PRACTICE

Saryna hopes to one day be a mighty hero like her father. She has chosen a katana sword to help defend her village. She isn't as strong or fast as Jad, but she is deadly with a weapon in her hands.

When you've finished this drawing, try having Saryna strike a new pose with her sword!

STEP 1

STEP 2

STEP 3

STEP 4

FINAL!

HIROTO

Through many years of practice and lots of hard work, Hiroto became a martial arts master. When faced with danger, he can defeat enemies in the blink of an eye. His fierceness and speed are legendary in his homeland.

When you've mastered this drawing, try giving Hiroto some ninjas to fight against!

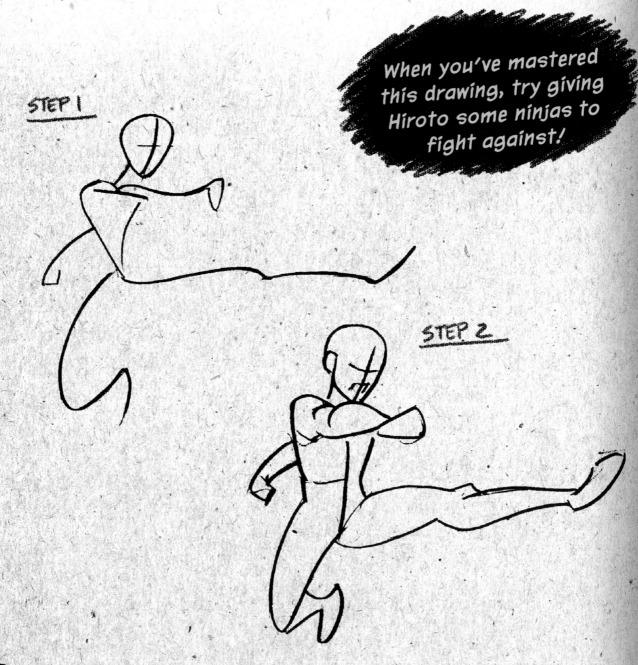

STEP 1

STEP 2

68

STEP 3

STEP 4

FINAL!

LINWEYA

Linweya has worked hard to become a master of the sword. She is a deadly foe with any blade. Luckily, she only uses her talents to defend the innocent. Like Hiroto, the people of her homeland are awed by her heroic deeds.

Once you've practiced this drawing, try giving Linweya some warriors to battle against!

STEP 1

STEP 2

STEP 3

STEP 4

FINAL!

MARAGI

Maragi is old—very old. Legends say he was once an evil wizard. As punishment, he was cursed to live forever. Now he teaches his students the honorable ways of the warrior code. He hopes to one day be released from his curse and finally be at rest.

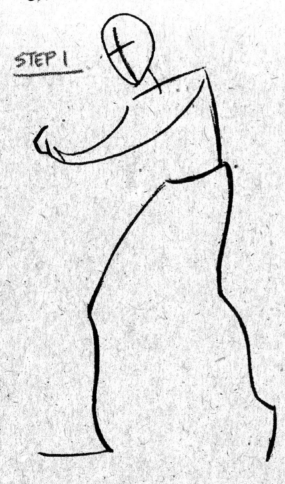

STEP 1

After practicing this drawing, try showing Maragi teaching new moves to a young warrior!

STEP 2

STEP 3

STEP 4

FINAL!

73

YUNA

Yuna is one of Maragi's best students. She is strong-willed, and often disobeys her parents. But with Maragi's teaching, Yuna is quickly becoming a highly skilled fighter. She is especially talented with her favorite weapon — the nunchucku.

When you're done with this drawing, try giving Yuna some new moves to use with her nunchucks!

STEP 1

STEP 2

STEP 3

STEP 4

FINAL!

GENERAL KUROK

The ways of the warrior will continue in the future. In the year 2235, General Kurok commands the battleship Blazing Arkon. Through studying history's greatest warriors, he has become the mightiest commander to ever travel the stars.

After you've practiced this drawing, try creating your own armor for General Kurok to wear!

STEP 1

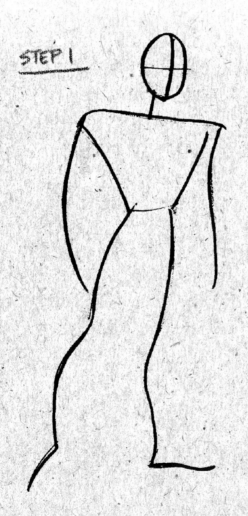

STEP 2

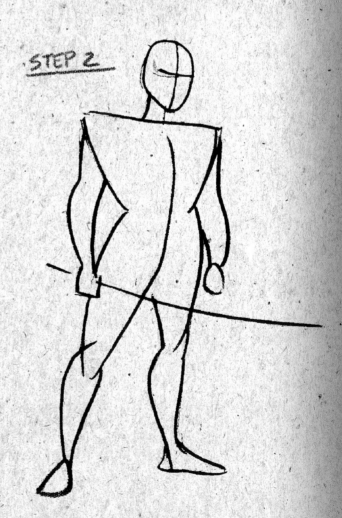

STEP 3

STEP 4

FINAL!

77

GHINSHU

Ghinshu is a master of the blade. He has fought in many battles in many lands. His body bears many scars, and he recently lost an eye battling a skilled foe. But in spite of his reduced vision, Ghinshu remains a deadly fighter with his sword.

After drawing Ghinshu, try drawing him again dueling another warrior!

STEP 1

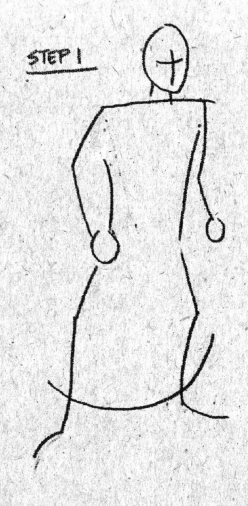

STEP 2

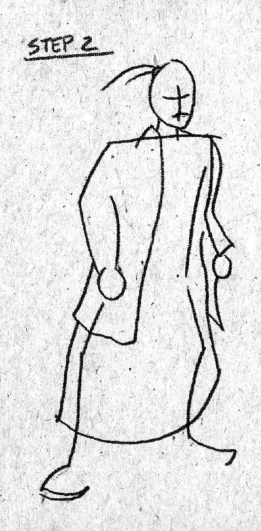

78

STEP 3

STEP 4

FINAL!

79

EPIC BATTLES

The Warriors of the Crescent Moon long fought against all injustice and evil. But one day the Black Emperor sent his emissary to dispose of those who stood against him. The epic battles between the warriors and the Black Emissary later became the stuff of legend.

This is just one possible scene from this battle. After you've drawn it, try your own poses and moves for these mortal enemies!

STEP 1

STEP 3

TO FINISH THIS DRAWING, TURN TO THE NEXT PAGE!

STEP 5

STEP 6

FINAL!

83

OTHER COOL STUFF

There are all kinds of awesome, cool things you can draw. You can have fun drawing comic book heroes and showing off their superpowers. Or you can draw big, ferocious dinosaurs and other animals eating their lunch. Or maybe you'd enjoy drawing ugly, gross monsters that scare people in their nightmares.

Whatever you think is cool, you can draw it! Try practicing the heroes, animals, dinosaurs, and monsters presented here. When you're done, get some fresh paper, and try drawing the coolest stuff you can imagine!

THUNDERFIST

Tired of being small and weak, Carl created a chemical formula to make him strong. Now he's called Thunderfist, and he can rip through concrete like it's cardboard. No crook can hide from this mountain of muscle!

After practicing this drawing, try showing Thunderfist blasting his way through a brick wall!

STEP 1

STEP 2

STEP 3

STEP 4

FINAL!

THE CREATURE

When criminals are on the loose, The Creature goes to work! His snarling face strikes fear into the hearts of criminals far and wide. When he's on the hunt, thugs can't escape his super sense of smell and tireless strength.

When you're done with this drawing, try showing The Creature sniffing out a big-time crook!

STEP 1

STEP 2

STEP 3

STEP 4

FINAL!

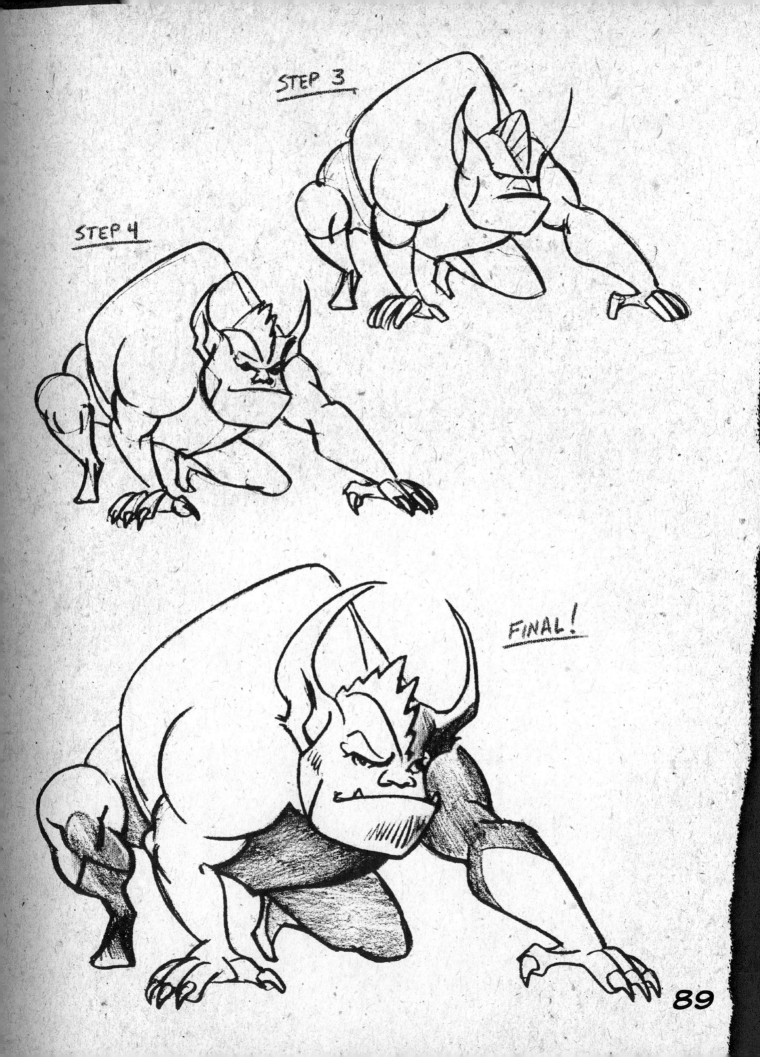

89

CAPTAIN ATMO

Captain Atmo is the world's most powerful hero. He's more than a mile tall and can pulverize mountains with his sonic fist blast. Whenever giant asteroids or alien ships threaten Earth, Captain Atmo is on the job!

After you've practiced this drawing, try showing Captain Atmo smashing an asteroid above the Earth!

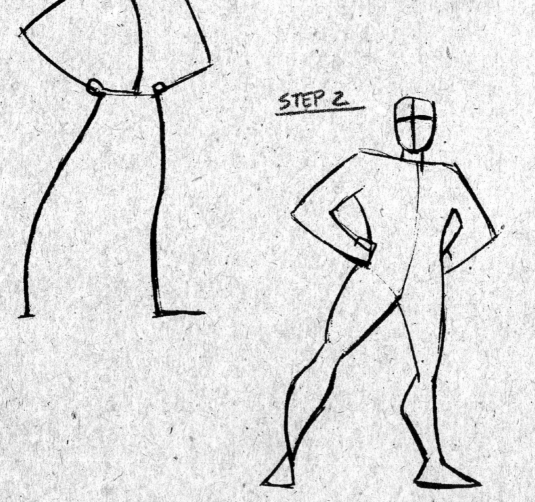

STEP 1

STEP 2

STEP 3

STEP 4

FINAL!

DRAGONFLY

Joe was a simple pilot dusting crops one day when his plane crashed. He survived, but he was soaked in chemicals. The next day he woke up with an extra pair of arms, superhuman strength, and he could run at incredible speeds. Now Joe fights crime as the world's newest hero—Dragonfly!

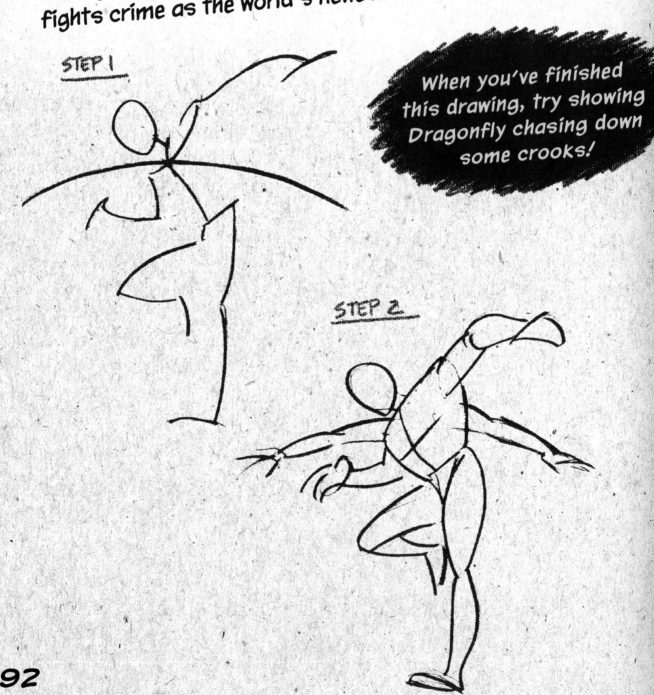

STEP 1

STEP 2

When you've finished this drawing, try showing Dragonfly chasing down some crooks!

STEP 3

STEP 4

FINAL!

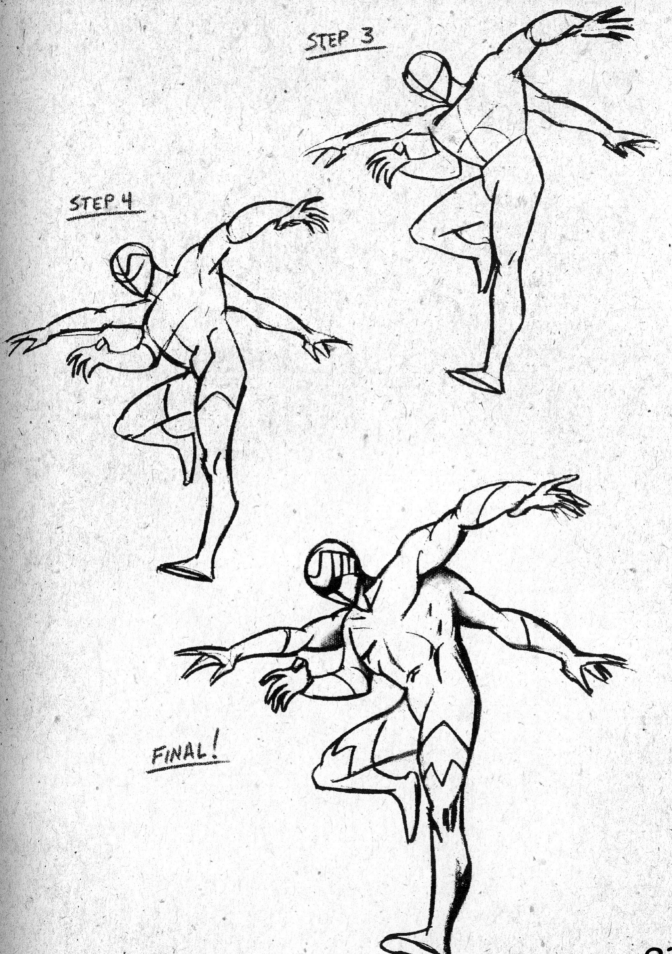

93

TEAM DYNAMO

As a team, the Dynamos have caught hundreds of thieves, muggers, and other thugs. They've also helped put away several major crime bosses. Along with their trusted family pet, Mighty Mutt, this hero team is feared by criminals around the world.

Once you've mastered Team Dynamo, try drawing them in action! What sorts of criminals would you like to see them fight?

STEP 1

STEP 2

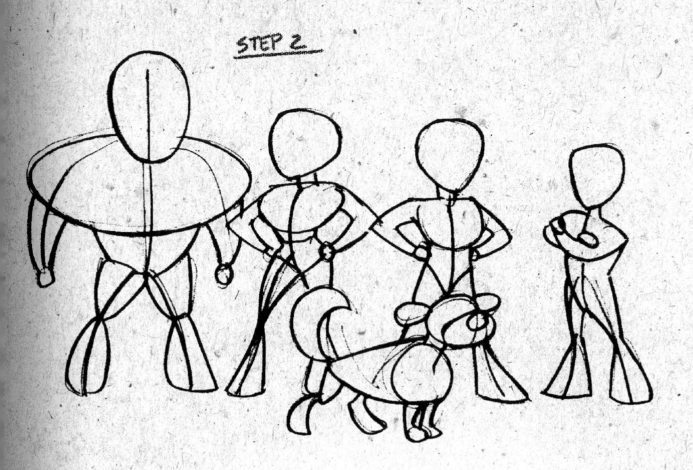

STEP 3

TO FINISH THIS DRAWING,
TURN TO THE <u>NEXT PAGE!</u>

STEP 4

STEP 5

STEP 6

FINAL!

97

GREAT WHITE SHARK

Great white sharks are ferocious predators. They grow to about 16 feet long. Their mouths often have as many as 3,000 sharp, jagged teeth. You don't want to come face-to-face with one of these huge "wolves of the sea!"

After drawing this shark, try drawing a bunch more in a feeding frenzy!

STEP 1

STEP 2

STEP 3

STEP 4

FINAL!

HIPPOPOTAMUS

Although a hippopotamus looks friendly, it's best to keep your distance. These massive 4,000-pound mammals can be very aggressive. And they can run faster than people for short distances. If you see one of these in the wild, be ready to quickly climb a tree!

When you're done drawing this beast, try showing a bunch of them grazing on the African plain.

STEP 1

STEP 2

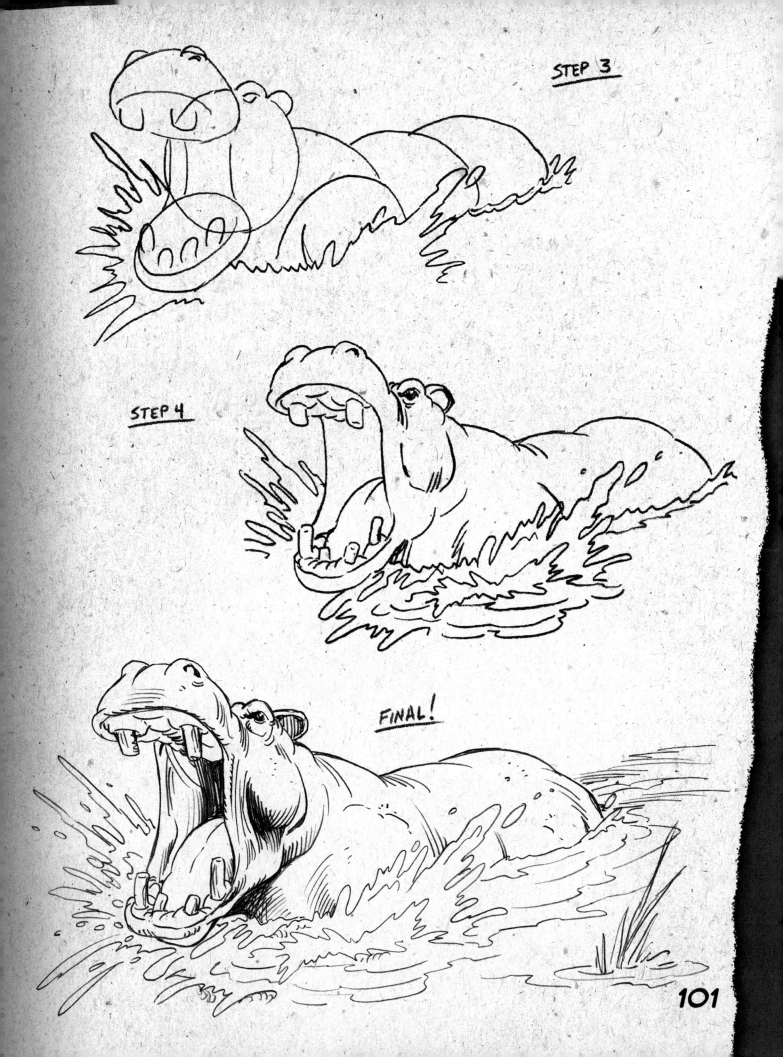

STEP 3

STEP 4

FINAL!

101

KOMODO DRAGON

At about 10 feet long and 350 pounds, Komodo dragons are the biggest lizards in the world. Their saliva is packed with deadly bacteria. Just one bite can infect and kill prey in just a few days. If you're ever in Indonesia, keep an eye out for these deadly reptiles!

After drawing this big lizard, try showing him swallowing his prey whole!

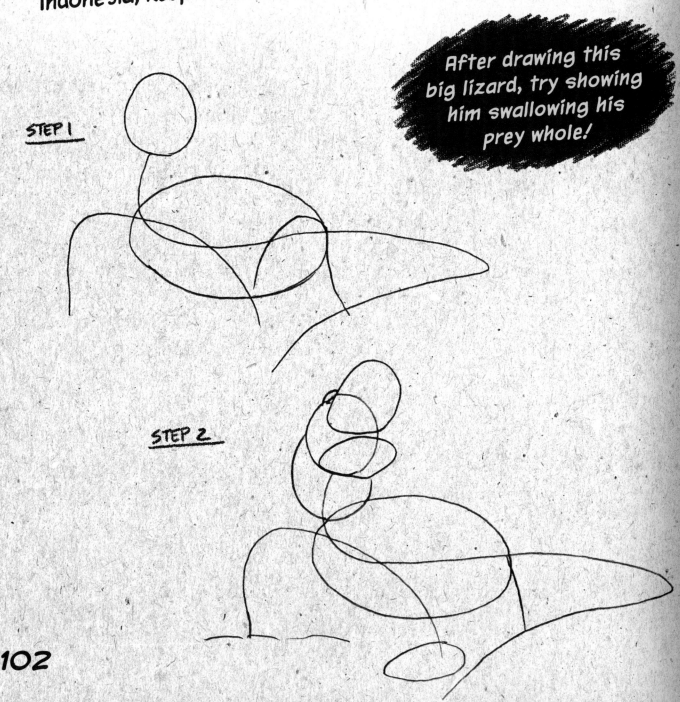

STEP 1

STEP 2

STEP 3

STEP 4

FINAL!

103

TIMBER WOLF

Wolves are the ancestors of dogs, but they're not man's best friend. They travel and hunt in packs, so if you see one, there are probably more wolves nearby. There is little to fear, though, because wolves rarely attack people. Just stay back, and they will leave you alone.

After drawing this wolf, try drawing a pack of them hunting an elk or moose!

STEP 1

STEP 2

STEP 3

STEP 4

FINAL!

105

BENGAL TIGER

Bengal tigers live mostly in India and Bangladesh. These big cats usually weigh about 500 pounds and are fierce predators. Their orange fur and black stripes help them hide in tall grass when hunting prey. They'll eat almost anything — even elephants!

After drawing this tiger, try showing it chasing down a water buffalo!

STEP 1

STEP 2

STEP 3

STEP 4

FINAL!

107

AFRICAN ELEPHANT

The African elephant is the largest land animal on Earth. These giant mammals can stand up to 12 feet tall and weigh as much as 22,000 pounds. If you see one of these charging at you, there's only one thing you can do — run!

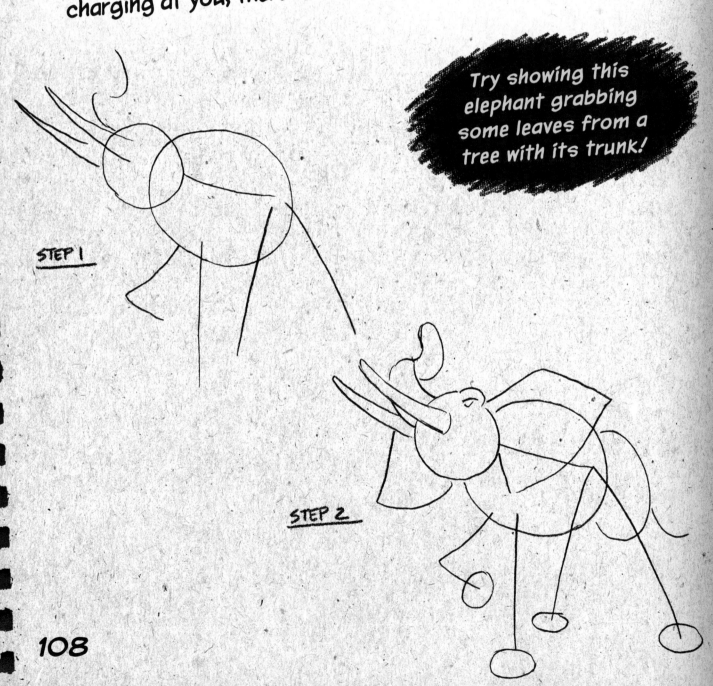

Try showing this elephant grabbing some leaves from a tree with its trunk!

STEP 1

STEP 2

STEP 3

STEP 4

FINAL!

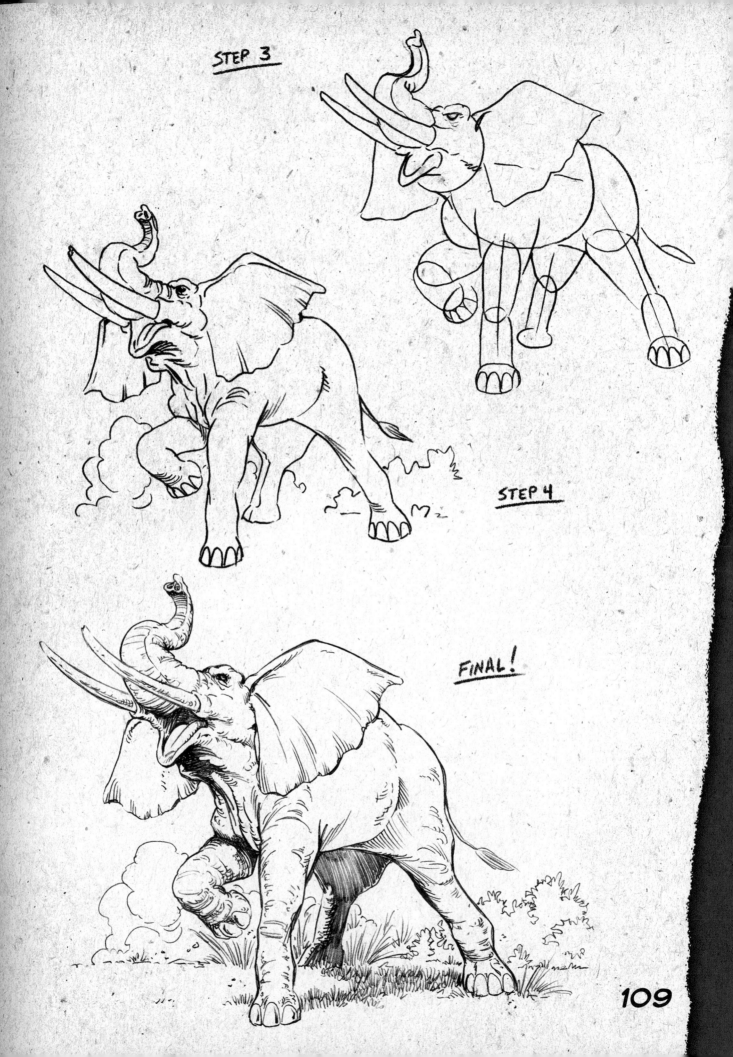

109

SALTWATER CROCODILE

Saltwater crocodiles are the largest reptiles living in the world today. These huge beasts can grow up to 23 feet long and weigh more than 3,300 pounds. Keep away from this monster, or it might think you'd make a tasty snack!

After drawing this big beast, try showing it lunging out of the water to grab its prey.

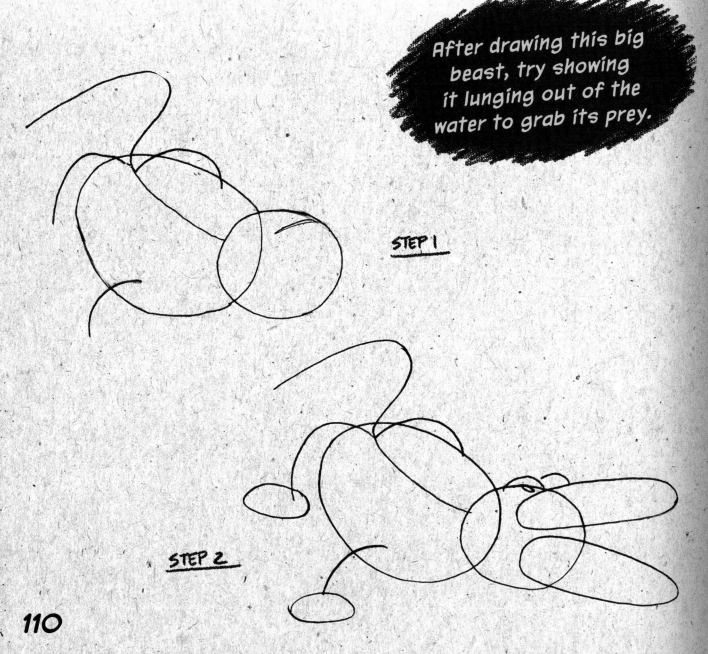

STEP 1

STEP 2

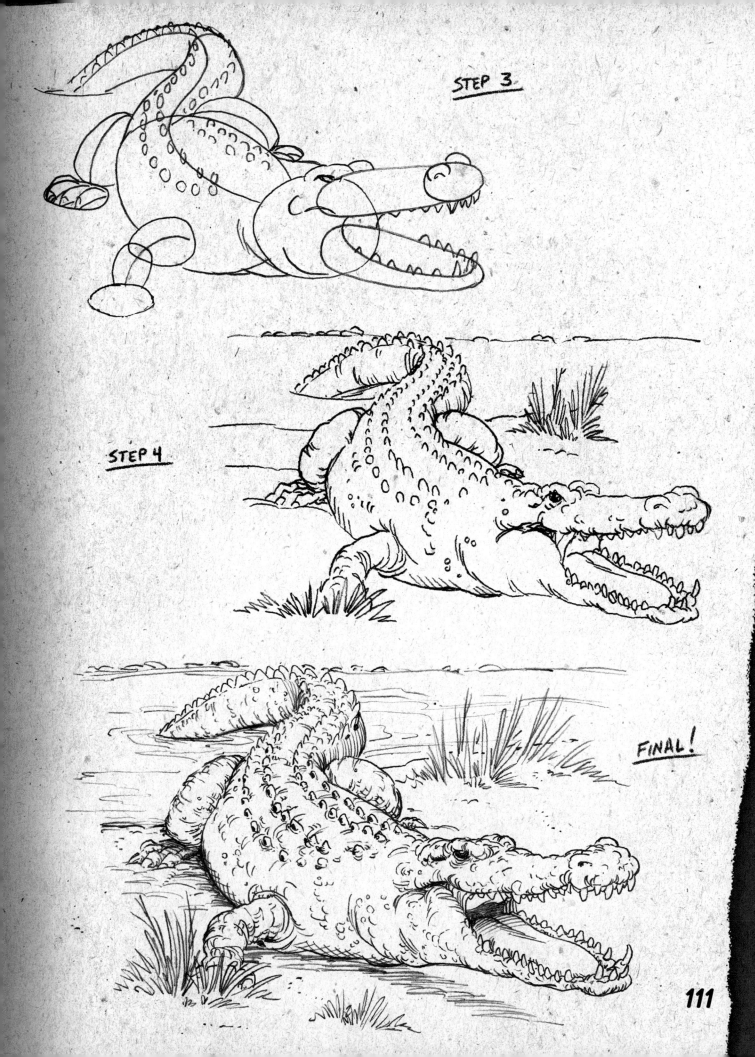

STEP 3

STEP 4

FINAL!

111

T-Rex Action!

The T-rex was a vicious hunter. It attacked other dinosaurs by ripping into them with its powerful jaws and huge back claws. Most creatures kept a sharp eye out for this fearsome predator.

After you've mastered the T-rex, try out the dinosaur fight on page 122!

STEP 1

STEP 2

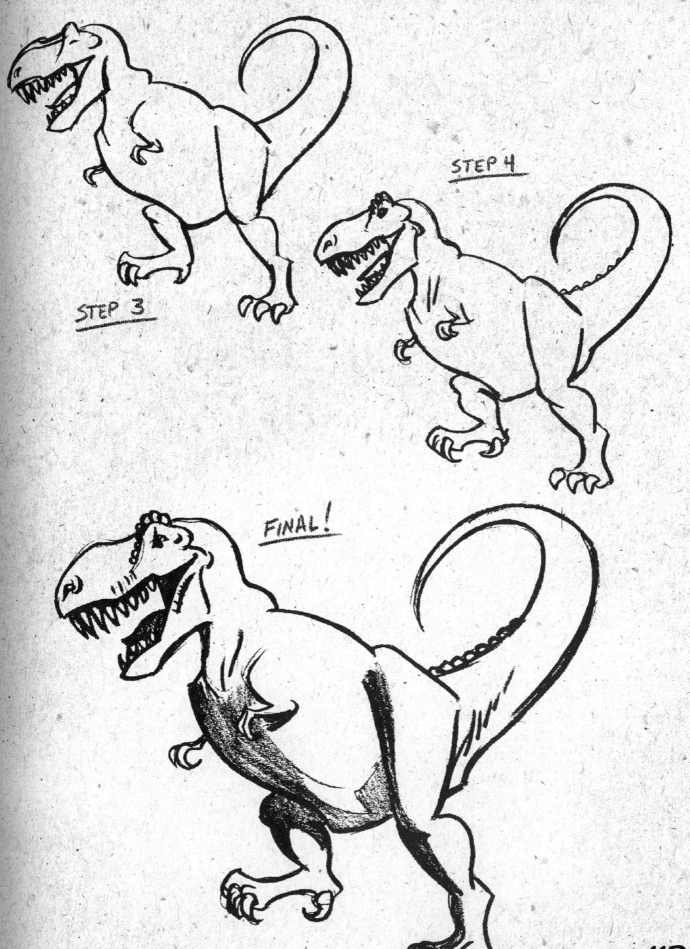

STEP 4

STEP 3

FINAL!

SPINOSAURUS

Even the mighty T-rex would have a hard fight against the gigantic Spinosaurus. This huge dinosaur was one of the biggest meat-eaters of all time. Even the spines on its back stood more than 6 feet tall. You definitely don't want this monster coming after you!

After you've practiced this vicious dinosaur, try putting him in a fight with a T-rex and see who wins!

STEP 1

STEP 2

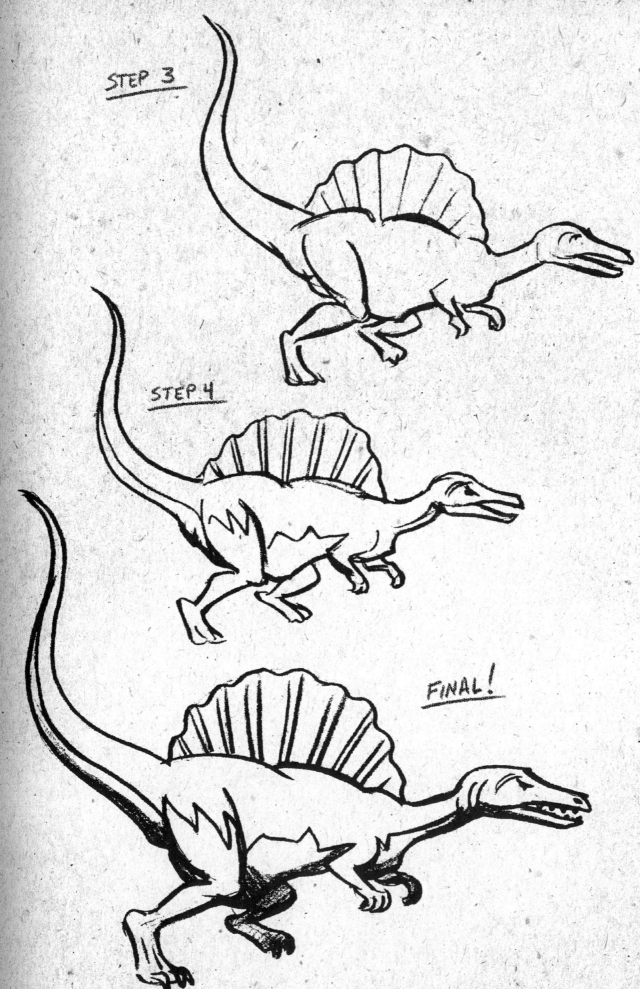

STEP 3

STEP 4

FINAL!

STEGOSAURUS

Watch out for that tail! Stegosaurus had a wicked defense against predators. Long, sharp spikes on the end of its tail kept enemies at a distance. Large back plates also kept hungry predators from chomping down on this dinosaur.

After drawing this dinosaur, try giving him some nasty battle scars from a fight!

STEP 1

STEP 2

STEP 3

STEP 4

FINAL!

117

TRICERATOPS

If the Triceratops charges, you'd better get out of the way fast! This dinosaur really lived up to its name, which means "three-horned face." It used its three large horns as an effective defense against predators.

STEP 1

Once you've practiced drawing this dinosaur, be sure to try out the dino fight on page 122!

STEP 2

STEP 3.

STEP 4

FINAL!

VELOCIRAPTOR

This creature looks strange, but don't be fooled. The Velociraptor was a fast and deadly hunter. It could run up to 40 miles per hour. Its wicked claws and needlelike teeth easily tore into its prey.

STEP 1

After drawing this vicious creature, try drawing a pack of them on the hunt for fresh meat!

STEP 2

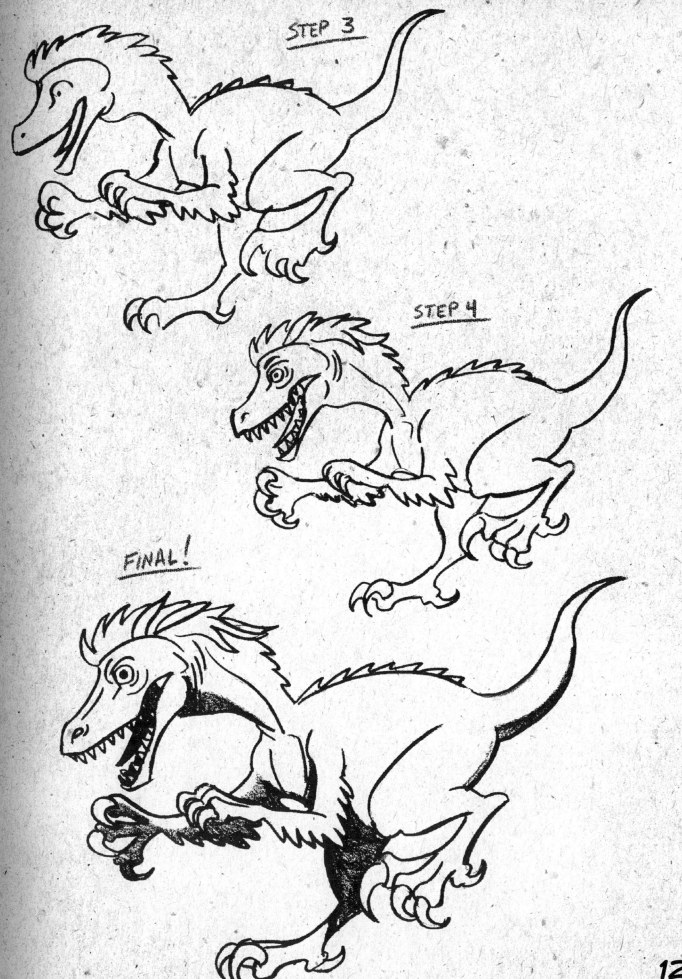

STEP 3

STEP 4

FINAL!

121

DINO FIGHT!

Don't get in the middle of this fight! One wrong move and the T-rex might decide that you'd be an easier meal. Or you might have to run from the Triceratops and his three huge horns. Which dino do you think will win?

Once you've mastered this dino fight, try it again with the other dinosaurs from this book.

STEP 1

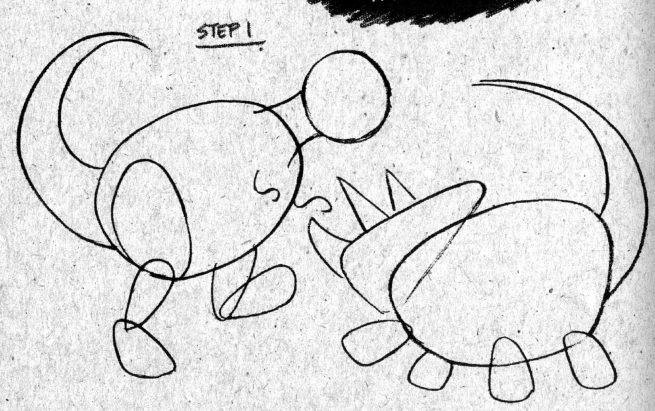

122

STEP 2

STEP 3

TO FINISH THIS DRAWING,
TURN TO THE **NEXT PAGE!**

STEP 4

STEP 5

124

STEP 6

FINAL!

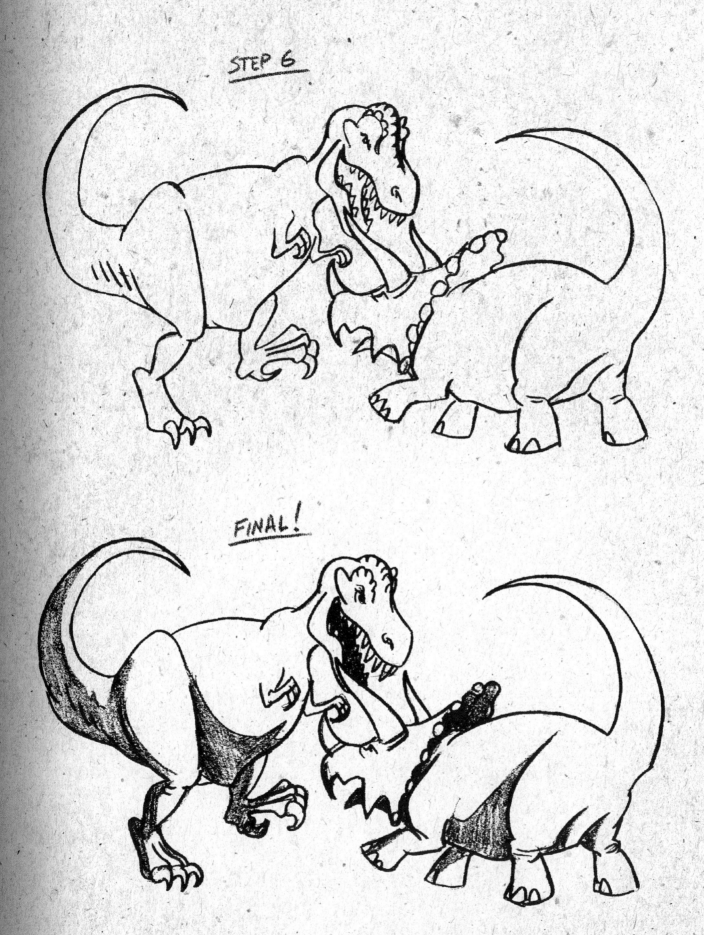

KRACKED KARL

Keep away from Kracked Karl the Krazy Klown! He was a simple circus clown who just wanted to make people laugh. But nobody thought he was funny. Now his mission is to make you laugh at his jokes — or else!

After drawing Karl, try giving him a crazy clown suit and some wacky balloons!

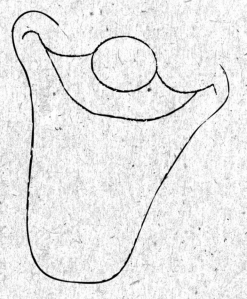

STEP 1

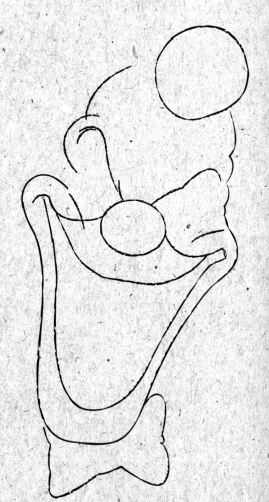

STEP 2

126

STEP 3

STEP 4

FINAL!

MEDUSA

Medusa was once a beautiful woman. All the young men adored her. But the Greek goddess Athena was jealous. She stole Medusa's beauty and changed her hair into hissing snakes. Afterward, any young man who looked at Medusa was turned to stone!

Try drawing Medusa's body. Does she have the body of a normal woman, or of a slippery snake?

STEP 1

STEP 2

STEP 3

STEP 4

FINAL!

129

SKELETAL SOLDIER

Even the bravest warriors tremble in fear when facing an army of Skeletal Soldiers! These undead creatures do not fear death. And they never stop fighting until their bones are smashed to bits.

After practicing this monster, try adding some armor or a bigger shield!

STEP 1

STEP 2

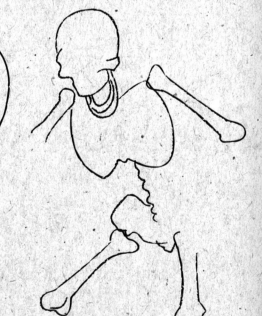

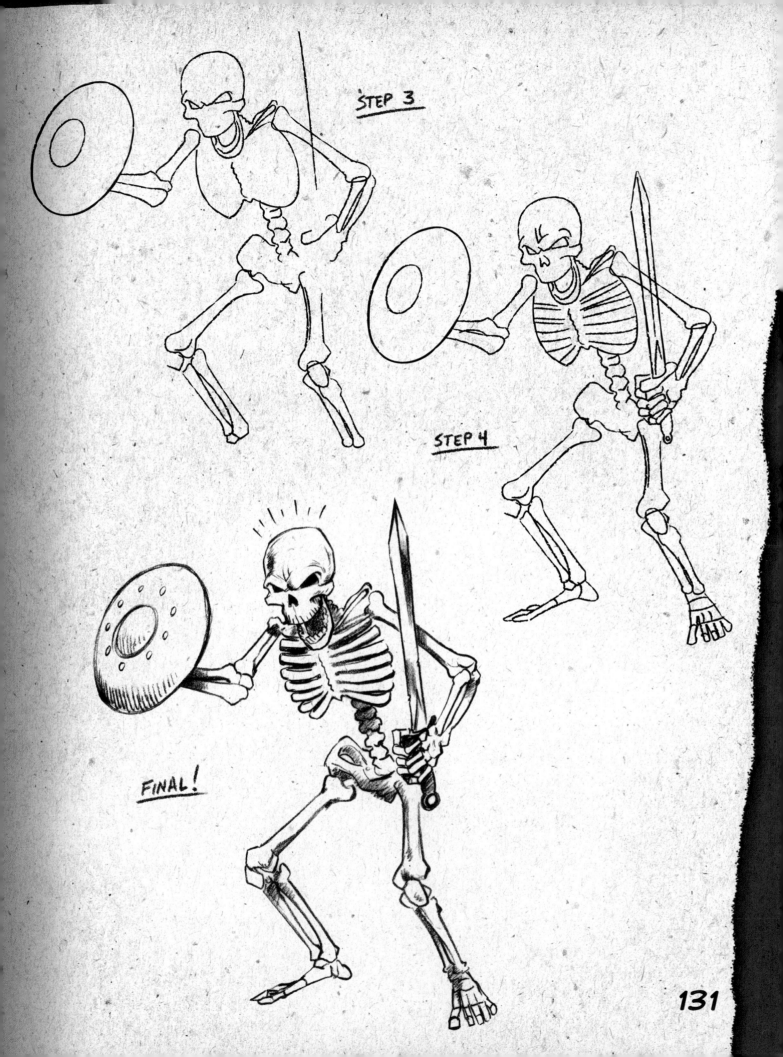

STEP 3

STEP 4

FINAL!

131

FRANK STEIN

Poor Frank Stein. Nobody understands him. He just wants to be everyone's friend. But people keep chasing him with pitchforks and torches. It's just not easy being 8 feet tall with green skin and bolts sticking out of your head!

After drawing Frank, try drawing him again dancing with his wife!

STEP 1

STEP 2

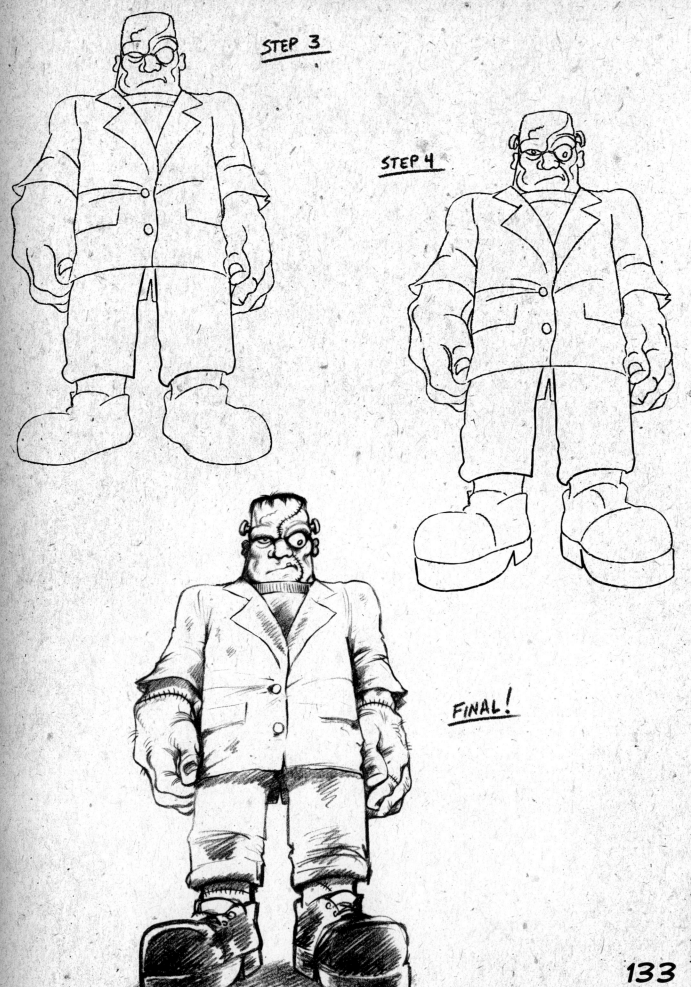

STEP 3

STEP 4

FINAL!

KING HOTEP

Who dares to disturb King Hotep's sleep? Watch out, this is one mad mummy! Even after a 3,000-year nap, Hotep still wakes up cranky. Quick, give him a glass of warm milk. Otherwise he might take you on a permanent vacation — to his tomb!

When you're done drawing this mummy, try showing him walking through a museum!

STEP 1

STEP 2

STEP 3

STEP 4

FINAL!

135

FISHY PHIL

Fishy Phil is a gruesome monster from the deep oceans. His huge eyes help him see in the dark depths. He easily catches prey with his sharp claws. Phil is also an excellent swimmer. You'd better run if you see his scaly head pop out of the water!

After drawing this scaly monster, try showing him catching some fish in the ocean!

STEP 1

STEP 2

STEP 3

STEP 4

FINAL!

137

UGH THE THUG

Ugh is a simple troll. It doesn't take much to make him happy. He loves to catch weary travelers crossing his bridge. Usually, he'll just take all their gold. But sometimes, he'll cook them for his dinner!

Try drawing Ugh in a tug-of-war with his brother Chugh over a bag of stolen gold!

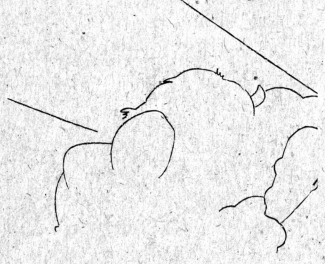

STEP 1

STEP 2

138

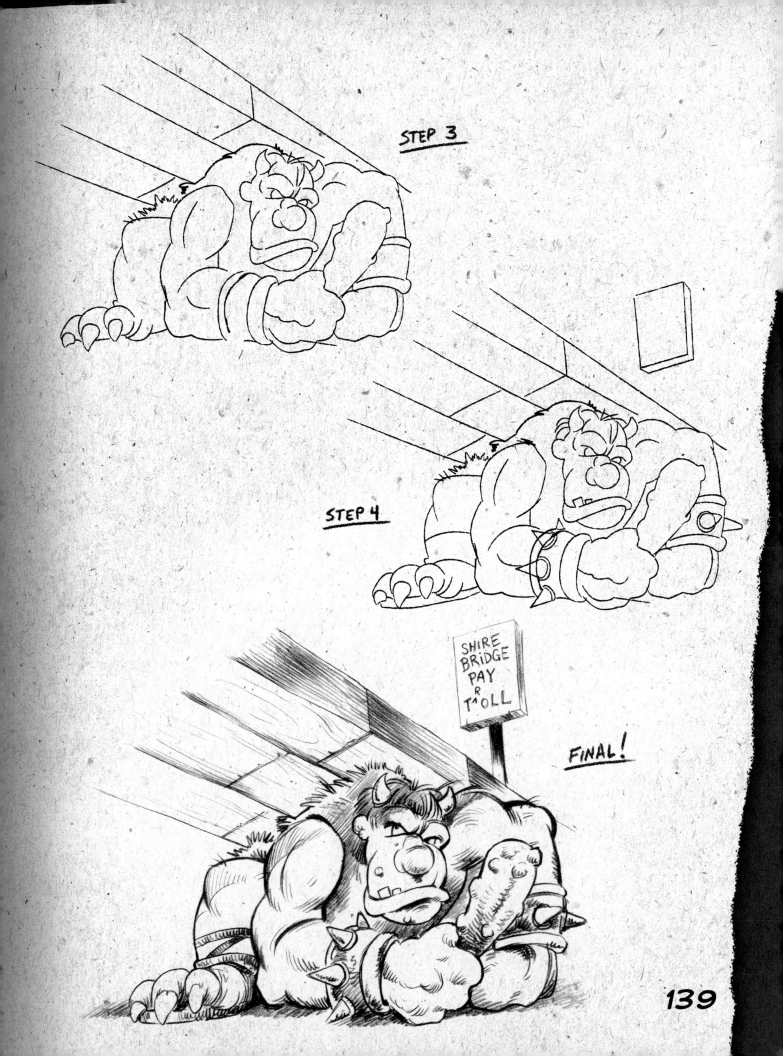

STEP 3

STEP 4

SHIRE
BRiDGE
PAY
R
TºOLL

FINAL!

139

MONSTER MASH!

Gigantic monsters always seem to be smashing the city of Tokyo, Japan. This time it's King Reptoid versus The Great Ape. Either one could win this brawl. King Reptoid has intense flaming breath, but The Great Ape has superior strength. It's anybody's guess what sorts of giant beasts will show up for Round 2!

After you've mastered this drawing, try it again with your own giant imaginary monsters!

STEP 1

140

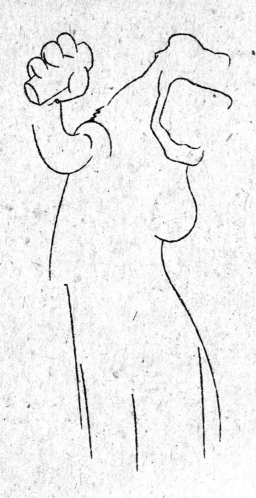

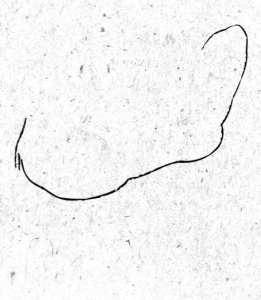

STEP 3

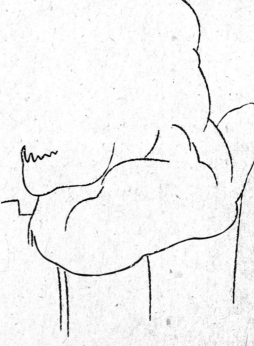

TO FINISH THIS DRAWING,
TURN TO THE NEXT PAGE!

STEP 4

STEP 5

STEP 6

FINAL!

143

Published by Capstone Press,
1710 Roe Crest Drive, North Mankato, Minnesota, 56003.
www.capstonepub.com

Library of Congress Cataloging-in-Publication Data
Sautter, Aaron.
    The boys' guide to drawing aliens, warriors, robots and other
cool stuff / by Aaron Sautter ; illustrated by Bob Lentz ... [et al.].
    p. cm.
    Summary: "Lively text and fun illustrations describe how to draw aliens,
warriors, robots, and other cool stuff." — Provided by publisher.
    ISBN-13: 978-1-4296-2917-1 (paperback)
    ISBN-10: 1-4296-2917-7 (paperback)
    ISBN-13: 978-1-4296-9896-2 (e-book)
    1. Drawing — Technique — Juvenile literature. I. Lentz, Bob. II. Title.
NC655.S28 2009
743'.89629892 — dc22   2008021997

Credits
Kyle Grenz, designer

Printed in China.
009952R